D1526081

The Red River Campaign

Union and Confederate
Leadership and the War in Louisiana

Editors

Theodore P. Savas, David A. Woodbury
and Gary D. Joiner

Parabellum Press

First Parabellum edition, 2003
1 2 3 4 5 6 7 8 9—05 04 03 02 01

ISBN 0-9726672-0-2

Cover image courtesy of Duke University, Durham, North Carolina.

Additional copies may be available at special discounts for bulk purchases in the U.S. For more information, contact: Parabellum Press, P.O. Box 44144, Shreveport, LA 71104. 318-222-6112 (phone); 318-222-0662 (Fax); gdjoiner@bellsouth.net (E-mail)

Edwin C. Bearss, Historian Emeritus, National Park Service, is the author of numerous books and articles, and a favorite Civil War speaker and tour guide.

Arthur W. Bergeron, Jr., historian at Pamplin Historical Park, is the author of many works, including *Guide to Louisiana Confederate Military Units* (LSU, 1989, 1996).

Gary D. Joiner owns Precision Cartographics and authored *One Damn Blunder From Beginning To End: The Red River Campaign of 1864* (Scholarly Resources, 2003). He is also a history professor at Louisiana State University in Shreveport.

Our friend *Charles Edmund "Eddie" Vetter*, the author of *Sherman: Merchant of Terror, Advocate of Peace* (Pelican, 1992), passed away suddenly in July 1994.

Theodore P. Savas, of Savas Publishing & Consulting Group, co-authored *Nazi Millionaires: The Allied Search for Hidden SS Gold* (Casemate, 2002), with Ken Alford.

Edward Steers, Jr., one of the country's foremost Lincoln experts, is the author of *Blood on the Moon: The Assassination of Abraham Lincoln* (UPK, 2001).

David A. Woodbury, co-founder of Savas Woodbury Publishers, is the Reprints Supervisor with Stanford University Press.

CONTENTS

MAPS AND PHOTOS

Tom Green's Battle at Blair's Landing *(National Archives)*

Edwin C. Bearss

Foreword–
On to the Red River!

$\mathcal{N}$ ot since the decade of the 1890s, when the veterans were a generation and a half removed from the Civil War, and the five "old War Department Parks" were established with their numerous unit and state memorials, has interest in "our" war been as pervasive. Since 1988, we have fought the "Eighth Battle of Manassas," been enlightened by the motion picture *Glory*, been challenged by Ken Bums' "The Civil War"—and applauded when it bested Monday Night Football in the television popularity ratings—hailed Ted Turner's *Gettysburg*, and watched the Arts & Entertainment Channel's Civil War Journal. The public's response to these mass media extravaganzas and preservation struggles has dramatically increased interest in the Civil War and battlefield preservation and education. This is reflected in the large number of visitors and crowded parking areas at most of the nation's Civil War battlefield parks, and the outpouring of publications—books, articles, compendiums, etc.—capitalizing on an apparently insatiable quest for information.

Reflecting the public's interest and concern for preservation and interpretation of Civil War sites, former Secretary of the Interior Manuel Lujan and Congress, under the leadership of former Senator Dale Bumpers of Arkansas and former Congressman Bruce Vento of Minnesota, in 1990-1991 established and funded the American Battlefield Protection Program. The Civil War Sites Study Commission was authorized by the Congress and in mid-July 1993 submitted its report. The Commission, while gathering information, held a number of public meetings in the field and visited battlefields in the Trans-Mississippi and Confederate Heartland, as well as in the Eastern Theater of the war. The Commissioners, the majority of whom came to the earlier meetings with an Eastern bias, soon came to appreciate the Western battlefield sites, their significance and integrity, and the commitment of the local people to their preservation and interpretation in a regional context.

The original decision by Savas Woodbury Publishers to highlight the Red River Campaign in the special issue of their heralded *Civil War Regiments* series was welcomed by Civil War students and buffs, as well as by the Commissioners and staff, the Commission having submitted its report and disbanded. For example, the Red River Expedition was identified by the Commission, along with the Shenandoah Valley Campaign of 1862-1864, as one of six major operations *not* represented in the National Park System. Three of the battles associated with the Red River Expedition—Mansfield, Pleasant Hill, and Fort De Russy—are among the ninety-six engagements found by the Commission to be Class A or B sites—battlefields of exceptional military importance. Sites and structures associated with Maj. Gen. Nathaniel P. Banks' Red River Expedition are increasingly becoming destinations for Civil War reenactors and battlefield stompers. Spearheaded by preservation groups, large parcels of property have been purchased from willing sellers and given to the state of Louisiana for inclusion in the Mansfield State Commemorative Area, more than tripling the area in public ownership. In the almost 40 years since the centennial commemoration held in 1964 on the Mansfield battlefield, at which the guest of honor was Prince Victor de Polignac, son of Confederate Brig. Gen. Camille Armand Jules Marie, Prince de Polignac, the New Orleans, Baton Rouge, and Houston Civil War Round Tables have campaigned through the Red River country with the "Bobbin Boy" from Waltham and his soldiers in blue or marched with Dick Taylor and his lean rugged butternuts.

This special publication, made available again by Parabellum Press, is just what the doctor ordered for Civil War readers interested in the Red River Expedition and its significance to the war as a whole. *The Red River Campaign: Union and Confederate Leadership in Louisiana* features three excellent monographs, collected letters written by a Union soldier to his wife, and a new helpful essay on touring the campaign's primary sites of interest.

Arthur W. Bergeron, Jr., one of the legendary T. Harry Williams' students, has long been recognized for research and writing skills that have made him an authority on the Civil War as it relates to Louisiana units and journals, Confederate Mobile, and lesser known Cajun country vignettes. Dr. Bergeron's introductory monograph entitled "Colonel Gains His Wreath: Henry Gray's Louisiana Brigade at the Battle of Mansfield, April 8, 1864" sets the tone of excellence for this collection. The author draws on an encyclopedic knowledge of Louisiana sources to introduce us to Colonel Gray, his command, and his officers and men. He then weaves the story of the brigade's "go for broke" charge that made Gray a brigadier general and tipped the scales against the

Federals at Mansfield. Bergeron keeps the battle in context without smothering the reader in detail and trivia—a common failing of many historians.

The next monograph, "The Union Naval Expedition on the Red River, March 12-May 22, 1864," is written by Gary D. Joiner and the late Charles E. Vetter. It singles out Rear Adm. David B. Porter and "Uncle Sam's webbfeet." Too often, the Union navy and its decisive role in many of the joint operations on Western waters is not given any recognition. On the Red River Expedition, the cooperation that ensured success when Maj. Gen. Ulysses S. Grant worked with Porter was missing. Porter and General Banks were like oil and water: they had divergent goals, thus ensuring the failure of the expedition. But for Lt. Col. Joseph Bailey, the navy might have left all if its ironclads on the Red River.

When I prepared the Foreword to the Red River Campaign issue in 1994, it was my initial association with Gary Joiner. Since then, Gary and my travels have crossed paths a number of times on Red River Civil War tours. These meetings demonstrated that in the past decade, Joiner, through his research and writings, has become an unsurpassed font of knowledge on naval and amphibious warfare in the Red River Basin. He is also the author of the long awaited *One Damn Blunder From Beginning To End: The Red River Campaign of 1864* (Scholarly Resources: Wilmington, Delaware), which is scheduled for release in early 2003.

I recall with sadness the first time I read Vetter's coauthored many years ago, because it was Eddie's last contribution to Civil war historiography. I first met Professor Vetter on a field trip to Vicksburg in the spring of 1989. I was impressed with his knowledge and enthusiasm. On Sunday, when the tour broke up, Eddie introduced me to several of his students from Centenary College, who had driven over from Shreveport to join him for several hours in the Vicksburg park. Then in the autumn of 1990, it was my pleasure to read and comment on Eddie's manuscript, *Sherman: Merchant of Terror*, *Advocate of Peace*, that was published by Pelican Publishing Company in 1992. The last time I saw my friend was in Wilmington, North Carolina, in October 1993, at Jerry Russell's 19th Civil War Round Table Congress. Also present were Sherman biographer John F. Marszalek and Craig L. Symonds, the author of the latest Joseph E. Johnston biography. What an experience it was to walk the Bentonville battlefield with this trio and share their thoughtful insights.

Theodore P. "Ted" Savas writes of "A Death at Mansfield: Colonel James H. Beard and the Consolidated Crescent Regiment," and demonstrates that he has a rare talent to successfully wear two hats. Besides being a publisher of first-class historical literature, he has authored an article that more than meets my personal criteria in defining a worthwhile contribution to what I need to know about the Civil War. It is written in an entertaining and graceful style; it draws in part on primary or little known secondary sources; and it is of general interest and adds substantially to what I know about events, sites, etc.

"Occupation," comprised of the letters written by Lt. Charles W. Kennedy of the 156th New York Volunteer Infantry to "My Dearest Katey," are of exceptional interest. Lieutenant Kennedy, as a staff officer in Brig. Gen. Cuvier Grover's division, did not get beyond Alexandria, Louisiana. He wrote to his wife, describing the Red River Campaign as it unfolded and as it was experienced by those at the front. This provides us with a different perspective and enables us to better appreciate what occurred in and around Alexandria, as the campaign that began with high hopes unraveled. Ed Steers—longtime friend, one of the founders of the Montgomery County, Maryland, Civil War Round Table, and Lincoln expert extraordinaire—merits kudos for bringing the Kennedy correspondence to our attention. Equally important is his ability to provide a succinct introduction to identify Lieutenant Kennedy and paragraphs where needed to lend context. In doing so, Ed Steers is not hamstrung by a failure all too common of editors tilting to extremes—either providing too much extraneous data or too little.

I welcome the decision to include in this revised edition Gary Joiner's "Touring The Red River Campaign," complete with several excellent maps of his own creation and modern photographs. Everyone who reads it will find it helpful, whether perusing it from an armchair far from the field or driving the highways of Louisiana in search of some of the most fascinating events of our own Civil War.

Arthur W. Bergeron, Jr.

A Colonel Gains His Wreath

Henry Gray's Louisiana Brigade
at the Battle of Mansfield, April 8, 1864

*T*he Battle of Mansfield, Louisiana, on April 8, 1864, was the turning point of the Red River Campaign. It was a bloody, hotly contested engagement that resulted in a stunning Confederate victory. Combined with a Union strategic defeat the next day at Pleasant Hill, Mansfield prompted the Federals to stop short their drive to capture Shreveport, their objective for the campaign. After these twin defeats, the Union columns retreated slowly back down the Red River to the Mississippi River, and safety.

Few of the Confederate soldiers who fought at Mansfield were Louisianians. Nearly three-quarters of the men in the Confederate army who fought there came from Texas. Nevertheless, a small Louisiana infantry brigade played a pivotal role in the battle and contributed greatly to the Confederate victory. No one has yet written a thorough story of what those Louisianians did during the April 8 engagement. Scattered sources and conflicting accounts have probably been the main reasons for this odd gap in the historical record. This essay attempts to fill that void by bringing together information from various sources and attempting to resolve some of the contradictory accounts.

Major General Nathaniel P. Banks began his Red River Campaign in mid-March 1864. His army of 18,000 men marched toward Alexandria from Brashear (now Morgan) City. At the same time, some 10,000 Federals under Brig. Gen. Andrew J. Smith and a fleet of 20 gunboats under Rear Adm. David D. Porter moved up Red River from the Mississippi to join Banks at Alexandria. Banks planned to move his force from that point to Shreveport, 130 miles northwest, and capture that city. Shreveport was not only the state capital of Louisiana but the headquarters of the Confederate Trans-Mississippi Department. Major General Richard Taylor, Confederate commander of the District of Western Louisiana, had the responsibility of opposing Banks and his powerful flotilla. It was a difficult assignment, for Taylor's army numbered only

6,000 men at the beginning of the campaign. Because the enemy's forces outnumbered his own so greatly, Taylor had to retreat from Alexandria past Natchitoches in the direction of Shreveport. General Edmund Kirby Smith, Taylor's superior, had ordered 2,500 to 3,000 cavalrymen from Texas and another 4,000 infantrymen from Arkansas to reinforce Taylor. Until these soldiers could reach him, Taylor had to avoid a major battle.[1]

The Texas cavalrymen began joining Taylor's army April 1-2 near Natchitoches, Louisiana. Although the infantrymen from Arkansas had managed to reach Shreveport by March 24, they did not join Taylor until April 8. Banks' army reached Natchitoches on April 2 and, to Taylor's surprise, began marching away from the Red River on a road that led through the towns of Pleasant Hill and Mansfield, a strategic blunder that carried the Federals away from the protection of Porter's gunboats. Taylor took advantage of Banks' mistake and selected a site at Moss Plantation, about three miles southeast of Mansfield, at which to fight the enemy. Because he expected the Confederates to continue retreating, Banks allowed his army to become strung out along the narrow road leading through the dense forest toward Mansfield.[2]

Taylor arranged his army of 8,800 men in battle formation and awaited the enemy. His force consisted of Maj. Gen. John G. Walker's Texas infantry division, three Texas cavalry brigades under Brig. Gen. Tom Green, and another small infantry division under the command of Brig. Gen. Alfred Mouton, which was composed of one Louisiana brigade and one Texas brigade. Brigadier General Camille J. Prince de Polignac, a Frenchman, led Mouton's Texas brigade, while Col. Henry Gray had charge of Mouton's three regiments, which composed the Louisiana brigade. Although records are woefully incomplete, Gray's command probably numbered little more than 1,000 men.[3]

A native of South Carolina, the 48-year-old Gray had been a prominent attorney and politician in Bienville Parish, Louisiana, prior to the war. He had

---

1 Ludwell H. Johnson, *Red River Campaign: Politics and Cotton in the Civil War* (Baltimore, 1958), pp. 99-100; U.S. War Department, *War of the Rebellion: The Official Records of the Union and Confederate Armies*, 128 vols. (Washington, D. C., 1880-1901), Series 1, Vol. 34, pt. 1, pp. 167-168, 657; pt. 2, pp. 879, 948. Hereinafter cited as *OR*. All citations are to Series 1; Richard Taylor, *Destruction and Reconstruction: Personal Experiences of the Late War*, ed, by Richard B. Harwell (New York, 1955), pp. 184-185,187. Johnson's seminal work should be the starting point for anyone who wishes to read or do research about the campaign.

2 *OR* 34, pt. 1, pp. 2, 84, 322, 324, 331, 428, 445, 513, 520, 563; Taylor, *Destruction and Reconstruction*, p. 190; Johnson, *Red River Campaign*, pp. 11 3,115.

3 *OR* 34, 1, p. 563.

Colonel Henry Gray

No uniformed photograph is known to exist.

organized the 28th Louisiana Infantry Regiment and became its colonel on May 17, 1862. Though he had no military experience, he trained his northern Louisiana farmers until they became well-disciplined and proficient in drill. Gray strongly disliked personal display and rarely wore a regular uniform distinguishing his rank. One of his soldiers recalled that Gray "was brave and fearless as a lion" and that he was "kind, careful of his soldiers, [and] attentive to their wants." The upcoming battle at Mansfield would earn the colonel a much deserved promotion to brigadier general.[4]

A trio of infantry regiments made up Gray's brigade: the 18th Consolidated, 28th Louisiana, and the Consolidated Crescent Regiment. The 18th Louisiana Consolidated regiment was formed on November 14, 1863, by combining the 18th Louisiana Regiment and the 10th (Yellow Jackets) Louisiana Battalion. Six companies of this new organization hailed from the 18th Louisiana and four

4   Arthur W. Bergeron, Jr., "Henry Gray," *The Confederate General*, William C. Davis, ed., 6 vols. (Harrisburg, 1991), vol. 3, pp. 26-27.

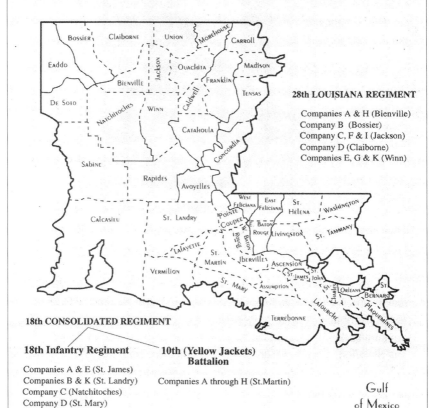

The Root Demographics of
Henry Gray's Louisiana Brigade

CONSOLIDATED CRESCENT REGIMENT

12th Infantry Battalion

Companies A & E (Rapides)
Companies B & C (Orleans)
Company D (St. Martin)
Company F (Lafourche)

24th Infantry

Companies A - K (Orleans)
Company L (Rapides)

11th Infantry Battalion

Companies A & D (DeSoto)
Companies B, C, & G (Natchitoches)
Company E (Sabine)
Company F (Catahoula)

28th LOUISIANA REGIMENT

Companies A & H (Bienville)
Company B (Bossier)
Company C, F & I (Jackson)
Company D (Claiborne)
Companies E, G & K (Winn)

18th CONSOLIDATED REGIMENT

18th Infantry Regiment

Companies A & E (St. James)
Companies B & K (St. Landry)
Company C (Natchitoches)
Company D (St. Mary)
Company F (Lafayette)
Company F (Lafayette)
Company G (Lafourche)
Companies H & I (Orleans)

10th (Yellow Jackets) Battalion

Companies A through H (St.Martin)

Gulf
of Mexico

LOUISIANA

from the Yellow Jackets Battalion. Most of the men were French-speaking Creoles and Cajuns from the southern part of the state. Combat was not new to these men. The members of the 18th Louisiana had been bloodied at the early April 1862 Battle of Shiloh and, along with the Yellow Jackets, had participated in the various battles and engagements of Taylor's army from October 1862 until the beginning of the Red River Campaign.[5]

Colonel Leopold Ludger Armant of St. James Parish led the 18th Consolidated at Mansfield. Armant was born in St. James Parish on June 10, 1835. He graduated from Georgetown College (University) in 1855 and from the University of Louisiana in 1858. After spending some time in Europe, Armant returned to his native parish to practice law and eventually served one term in the state legislature prior to the war. The Louisiana native joined the St. James Rifles as a second lieutenant and was promoted to first lieutenant when his unit became Company A of the 18th Louisiana. He was promoted to colonel on May 10, 1862, after the reorganization of the regiment.[6]

Neither of Armant's immediate subordinates, Lt. Col. Joseph Collins or Maj. William Mouton, participated in the first phase of the battle. Neither did either officer have any prewar experience. Lieutenant Colonel Collins, Armant's second in command, was born in New Orleans in 1837 and attended Spring Hill College near Mobile, Alabama. Before the war he was a bookkeeper for a dry goods company and a partner in a firm that ran a cotton press. Collins became captain of the Orleans Cadets on June 19, 1861, which joined the 18th Louisiana as Company I in January 1862. He was promoted to lieutenant colonel on May 10 of that year when the regiment was reorganized. After the war, Collins returned to his business pursuits and held several positions in the city government.[7]

---

5   For a detailed profile of the 10th Louisiana Battalion, see Arthur Bergeron, Jr., "The Yellow Jackets: The 10th Louisiana Infantry Battalion," *Civil War Regiments*, vol. 3, No. 1 (Spring, 1993), pp. 1-30. For an in-depth examination of the structure of Louisiana organizations, see Arthur W. Bergeron, Jr., *Guide to Louisiana Confederate Military Units, 1861-1865* (Baton Rouge, 1989), pp. 117-119,163-164.

6   "John S. Armant" and "Leopold L. Armant," in Glenn R. Conrad, ed., *Dictionary of Louisiana Biography*, 2 vols. (Lafayette, 1988), vol. 1, p. 19.

7   *New Orleans Daily Picayune*, April 5, 6,1886; Arthur W. Bergeron, Jr., ed., *Reminiscences of Uncle Silas: A History of the Eighteenth Louisiana Infantry Regiment* (Baton Rouge, 198 1), p. 229. Joseph Collins remained with half of the regiment as the brigade reserve when the attack began. His men did not move forward until after the enemy had been driven back from their first position from behind the fence line. Collins died at his home on April 4, 1886, and was buried in Metairie Cemetery. Ibid.

Colonel Armant's other field officer, William Mouton, was born on June 21, 1831, in St. Landry Parish. Mouton graduated from Yale University and opened a law practice in Vermilionville (now Lafayette), Louisiana. The prewar attorney entered Confederate service as a first lieutenant of the Acadian Guards and became its captain when it joined the 18th Louisiana as Company F. He was promoted to major when the regiment was reorganized on May 10, 1862.[8]

The second regiment in Colonel Gray's Brigade at Mansfield was Gray's own 28th Louisiana Infantry Regiment, which was organized at Monroe, Louisiana, in April 1862. Its soldiers hailed from the rural northern areas of the state. They had fought in the battles of Fort Bisland and Irish Bend in April 1863, and followed the marches of Mouton's Brigade from that time until the Battle of Mansfield. When Mouton was promoted to divisional command during the summer of 1863, Gray, as its senior colonel, succeeded Mouton in command of the brigade—without the addition of a collar wreath around his stars. Gray's advancement to brigade command left Lt. Col. William Walker in charge of the 28th Louisiana. A native of Alabama, Walker was born in 1832 and later moved to what became Winn Parish, Louisiana. The infantry company he raised after the war began became part of the 28th Louisiana, and Walker was elected lieutenant colonel of the regiment.[9]

There is some uncertainty about the role that Walker's subordinate, Maj. Thomas W. Pool, played at Mansfield. Most accounts state that every field officer who participated in the initial charge on the Union position was killed or mortally wounded. Pool received no wounds in the battle, so he may not have participated in the first phase of the fighting. A postwar account, however, claims that during the fighting Pool's "sword and pistol were shot from his side." The major was born in Perry County, Alabama, in August 1832 and grew up in

---

8   J. Franklin Mouton, III (comp. & ed.), *The Moutons: A Genealogy* (Lafayette, 1978), p. 16; Harry Lewis Griffin, *The Attakapas Country: A History of Lafayette Parish, Louisiana* (Gretna, 1974), p. 44; Rev. Donald J. Hebert, ed., *Southwest Louisiana Records: Church and Civil Records*, vol. 17, 1885-1886 (Cecilia, 1978), p. 452; Bergeron, *Reminiscences of Uncle Silas*, p. 231-232. William Mouton was absent sick during the Battle of Mansfield. After the war, he resumed his law practice and died on January 19, 1885, in New Iberia, Louisiana.

9   Bergeron, *Guide to Louisiana Confederate Military Units*, p. 138; Eighth Census of the United States, 1860; Population Schedules, Winn Parish, National Archives; Compiled Service Records of Confederate Soldiers Who Served in Organizations from the State of Louisiana, NA Microfilm No. 320, Roll 352; *Biographical and Historical Memoirs of Northwest Louisiana*, n.a. (Nashville, 1890), p. 492; Dale and Eugene F. Love, *Looking Back: Winn Parish, 1852-1986*, 2 vols. (Winnfield, 1986), 2, p. 131.

Union County, Arkansas, before moving to Claiborne Parish, Louisiana, in 1851. Soon thereafter Pool became a merchant in the town of Vienna. When the war began he raised a company in Jackson Parish and took it to Monroe, where upon its organization he was elected major of the 28th Louisiana.[10]

The last regimental element in Gray's Brigade was the Consolidated Crescent Regiment, formed by joining the Crescent (24th Louisiana) Regiment with the 11th and 12th (Confederate Guards Response) Louisiana Infantry battalions on November 3, 1863. Both the Crescent Regiment and the Confederate Guards Response Battalion (12th) had been organized in New Orleans as militia units in late 1861 and then transferred to Confederate service in March 1862. The men of these units had received their baptism of fire at Shiloh before joining Taylor's army in the early fall of 1862. The 11th Louisiana Battalion was organized at Monroe in May 1862, but had seen no real fighting prior to the Red River Campaign.[11]

The Crescent Regiment was commanded by a trio of capable, experienced officers: Col. James Beard of Shreveport, Lt. Col. Franklin H. Clack, and Maj. Mercer Canfield. The Crescent's commander, James Hamilton Beard, organized and became captain of the Shreveport Greys on January 17, 1861. When the battalion disbanded in Virginia in the spring of 1862, Beard returned to Shreveport and became major of the 11th Louisiana Infantry Battalion on May 14, 1862. He was promoted to lieutenant colonel three months later. His colonelcy dated from the formation of the Consolidated Crescent Regiment.[12]

Beard's subordinates were also longstanding veterans. Forty-six-year-old Florida native Franklin Hutze Clack, the son of a naval officer, was born April 4, 1828, in Pensacola. Raised in Norfolk, Virginia, he attended Princeton University and graduated from Yale Law School before moving to New Orleans in 1851, where he formed a law firm. For a brief period prior to the outbreak of Civil War he served as the city attorney for New Orleans. After serving as first lieutenant of Company D, Confederate Guards Regiment, Louisiana Militia, he was promoted to major at the organization of the Confederate Guards Response

10 *Biographical and Historical Memoirs of Northwest Louisiana*, p. 446.

11 Bergeron, *Guide to Louisiana Confederate Military Units*, pp. 130-132, 146-147, 164-166.

12 Compiled Service Records of Confederate Soldiers Who Served in Organizations from the State of Louisiana, National Archives Microfilm No. 320, Roll 97. For a full account of the life and wartime service of James H. Beard, see, Theodore P. Savas, "A Death at Mansfield: Col. James H. Beard and the Consolidated Crescent Regiment," printed elsewhere in this issue.

Battalion on March 6, 1862. Clack was bumped up to lieutenant colonel shortly after the addition of several companies to the battalion in the fall of that year.[13]

The third field officer of the Consolidated Crescent was Maj. Mercer Canfield, a 26-year-old prewar lawyer from Alexandria. Canfield enlisted in the Red River Rebels as a second lieutenant on August 3, 1861, and became first lieutenant just two weeks later when that unit joined the 1st Louisiana Infantry as Company B. After his commission expired the following spring, Canfield returned home and raised a company of mounted rangers, which organized and entered service on July 4, 1862. The rangers were dismounted and became Company A, 12th Louisiana Infantry Battalion, on September 20. The young Louisianan was promoted to major of the battalion shortly after his company joined it.[14]

Major General Nathaniel Banks' army began its advance inland from Natchitoches and away from Red River on April 6, 1864.[15] Brigadier General Albert L. Lee's three brigades of cavalry led the column, followed by a train of supply wagons. Next in line came the men of Thomas E. G. Ransom's XIII Corps and a division of the XIX Corps led by William H. Emory, with the army's main supply trains bringing up the rear. The veteran troops of Andrew J. Smith's XVI Corps made up the rear guard, which did not leave the vicinity of Natchitoches until the following day. It did not take long before Lee's cavalry began running into Confederate opposition, when Federal troopers began skirmishing with Taylor's mounted arm early on April 7. Cavalry elements of both armies fought a brief engagement that afternoon at Wilson's Farm, about three miles north of Pleasant Hill. After two hours of indecisive fighting the Confederates, under the capable command of Brig. Gen. Tom Green, withdrew slowly toward Mansfield.[16]

---

13   Newspaper article (n.d.), Louisiana Historical Association Collection, Manuscripts and University Archives Division, Special Collections, Howard-Tilton Memorial Library, Tulane University, New Orleans; Compiled Service Records, Roll 374.

14   Compiled Service Records, Rolls 73, 281. This author has never seen any estimates of the strengths of the regiments in Gray's Brigade at Mansfield.

15   For background information on the evolution of the 1864 Red River Campaign, see, Gary D. Joiner and Charles E. Vetter, "The Union Naval Expedition on the Red River, March 12-May 22, 1864," printed elsewhere in this issue.

16   *OR* 34, pt. 1, p. 114, 168, 181, 198-199, 237, 256-257, 450, 478-480, 485, 519-520, 523, 526, 528, 563, 606, 616; Johnson, *Red River Campaign*, pp. 124-125. Albert Lee's cavalry brigades were commanded by Thomas J. Lucas (1st Brigade), Harai Robinson (3rd Brigade), and Nathan A. M. Dudley (4th Brigade). See Frank J. Welcher, *The Union Army, 1861-1865. Organization and Operations*, Volume 2, *The Western Theater* (Bloomington, 1993), pp. 763-765 for an order of battle.

The bulk of the Union army reached Pleasant Hill during the afternoon of April 7, where it went into camp. Wisely, Lee requested infantry reinforcements because of the stiff resistance he had met at Wilson's Farm. Although Maj. Gen. William B. Franklin, commanding the XIX Corps, refused to send assistance without additional orders, Banks directed him to support the cavalry vanguard with troops from the XIII Corps. As Frank Emerson's brigade, William J. Landram's division, prepared to march to Lee's assistance, Richard Taylor decided to make his stand against Banks the following day south of Mansfield. As a result of this decision, he ordered part of his cavalry to fall back to the position he had selected on the grounds of the Moss Plantation, while the remaining regiments remained at Ten Mile Bayou in order to contest and delay the expected Federal advance on the morning of April 8. Taylor also issued orders for the Arkansas and Missouri troops at Keatchie, about fifteen miles up the main road from Mansfield, to march to Moss Plantation.[17]

Alfred Mouton's Division, which had been camped about five miles north of Mansfield since April 4, broke camp at 6:30 a.m. four days later and marched through town to its new position on the Moss Plantation. Mouton's line on the Moss grounds was laid out on a small hill or ridge at the edge of a pine forest. Across the entire front of these Confederates was a large open field bisected by a split-rail fence. The field had been used to grow wheat, but nothing was growing in it at the time of the battle. On the other side of the field was one end of a slight ridge known as Honeycutt Hill. A narrow band of pine woods covered the hill. Across it, running roughly southeast to northwest, was a dirt road leading to Mansfield. Henry Gray's Louisiana brigade was deployed on the left flank of Mouton's two-brigade division, which was itself posted on the far left of Taylor's small infantry force, making Gray's Brigade, at least initially, the anchor for Taylor's extreme left flank. Gray's line was organized with the 28th Louisiana on the left, the 18th Louisiana in the center, and the Crescent Regiment on the right. Camille Polignac's brigade, deployed on Gray's right, held the right-front of Mouton's battle line. As elements of Green's Confederate cavalry retreated toward Mansfield in front of the advancing Union army, several of the regiments took up positions to the left of Gray's brigade, further extending the line and thus becoming the army's extreme left flank.[18]

17 *OR* 34, pt. 1, pp. 257, 294,526,563; Johnson, *Red River Campaign*, p. 131.

18   J. E. Hewitt, "The Battle of Mansfield, La.," *Confederate Veteran*, 40 vols. (1925), vol. 33, p. 172; Napier Bartlett, *Military Record of Louisiana* (Baton Rouge, 1964), "The Trans-Mississippi," p. 61; Edwin C. Bearss, ed., *A Louisiana Confederate: Diary of Felix Pierre Poche* (Natchitoches, 1972), pp. 104-106.

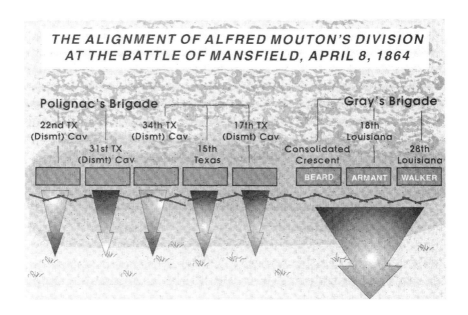

THE ALIGNMENT OF ALFRED MOUTON'S DIVISION
AT THE BATTLE OF MANSFIELD, APRIL 8, 1864

Polignac's Brigade   Gray's Brigade

22nd TX   34th TX   17th TX   18th
(Dismt) Cav   (Dismt) Cav   (Dismt) Cav   Louisiana
      31st TX   15th   Consolidated   28th
      (Dismt) Cav   Texas   Crescent   Louisiana

                                              BEARD   ARMANT   WALKER

About noon, Colonel Gray began extending his line further to the left to accommodate more men on his right. As this shift was underway, blueclad troopers from Union Col. Thomas J. Lucas' 1st Cavalry Brigade emerged from the woods across the field and made their presence known. Lucas' cavalrymen were only a short distance ahead of Col. Nathan A. M. Dudley's 4th Cavalry Brigade and Col. Frank Emerson's 1st Brigade, Fourth Division, XIII Corps. These inquisitive Federals had been slowly pursuing the Confederate rear guard since early that morning. The battle was about to begin.[19]

*   *   *

Initially, Gray's men did not realize that Colonel Lucas' cavalrymen were the enemy until they were only two hundred yards away. Mouton, who happened

---

19   Lucas' brigade consisted of the 16th Indiana Mounted Infantry, 2nd Louisiana Mounted Infantry, 6th Missouri Cavalry, 14th New York Cavalry regiments, and an attached howitzer battery under the command of Capt. Herbert Rottaken. The 2nd Illinois Cavalry, 3rd Massachusetts Cavalry, 31st Massachusetts (Mounted) Infantry, and 8th New Hampshire (Mounted) Infantry composed Dudley's brigade. Frank Emerson's brigade consisted of the 77th Illinois, 19th Kentucky, 67th Indiana, and 23rd Wisconsin regiments. *OR* 34, pt. 1, pp. 169, 171.

to be near the men at this time, quickly ordered the 18th Louisiana to halt its movement and open fire. A couple of volleys proved sufficient to drive the probing Federals back in some disorder, a small victory that inspired enthusiasm among the Confederates. Mouton rode up to the front lines, raised himself to full height in his stirrups, and waved his hat in his hand, yelling "Louisiana has drawn the first blood today, and the victory is ours!"[20]

At Mouton's request, the men of the brigade followed his lead and offered three cheers in response. Shortly thereafter, General Taylor appeared, along the front of the 18th's line to compliment the men on their conduct. Taylor described the event after the war in his memoirs. "Riding along the line, I stopped in front of the Louisiana brigade of Mouton's division, and made what proved to be an unfortunate remark to the men: 'As they were fighting in defense of their own soil I wished the Louisiana troops to draw the first blood.'" He continued: "At this moment our advanced horse came rushing in, hard followed by the enemy. A shower of bullets reached Mouton's line, one of which struck my horse, and a body of mounted men charged up to the front of the 18th Louisiana."[21]

Brigadier General Albert L. Lee, Banks' cavalry commander and the leader of the army's advance on April 8, brought up Colonel Emerson's infantry brigade and formed it into a line of battle on both sides of the Pleasant Hill–Mansfield Road. Lee deployed Dudley's cavalry brigade on Emerson's left and Lucas' troopers on his right. The Federals arranged their line at the edge of the field one-half to three-quarters of a mile distant from the Confederates. Both sides sent small parties of men into the open field to skirmish with each other. As one Louisiana captain back at the main line later remembered it, for the next few hours enemy bullets fell among the men like hail.[22]

Another officer recalled that during the protracted skirmishing in the field, Colonel Armant and several of his subordinates were sitting or lying in the

20   *OR* 34, pt. 1, pp. 265, 290-291, 450-451; Col. Henry Gray to Maj. E. Surget, April —, 1864, typescript at the Mansfield State Commemorative Area Museum; Bartlett, *Military Record of Louisiana*, p. 61; S. A. Poche, "Battle of Mansfield" (photocopy of unidentified newspaper clipping, Mansfield State Commemorative Area Museum); Bearss, ed., *A Louisiana Confederate*, p. 106.

21   Richard Taylor, *Destruction and Reconstruction*, p. 195; Bearss *A Louisiana Confederate*, 106.

22   *OR* 34, pt. 1, pp. 265, 291, 451; Entry of April 8, 1864, Arthur W. Hyatt Diary, Arthur W. Hyatt Papers, Louisiana and Lower Mississippi Valley Collection, Special Collections, Louisiana State University Library, hereinafter cited as Hyatt Diary; Poche, "Battle of Mansfield"; Bearss, *A Louisiana Confederate*, p. 106; Gray to Surget, April —, 1864.

woods behind the line of battle. Several stray bullets flew over their heads as Armant rested on the ground, his head supported by his hand. One minie ball struck the earth under his arm and threw dirt on his new uniform, prompting the colonel to stand up and brush it off, saying that he may die during the day but did not want his new coat soiled beforehand. Within two hours, Armant would lay dead on the battlefield, his new uniform stained with his blood.[23]

About midmorning, Union General Albert Lee asked for reinforcements to replace the fatigued soldiers of Colonel Emerson's brigade. Brigadier General Thomas E. G. Ransom, the commander of the XIII Corps, moved Col. William J. Landram's 2nd Brigade, which was led by Col. Joseph W. Vance, to Lee's assistance.[24] Vance's soldiers reached the field around 1:30 p.m. and took a position on the right of Emerson's men, directly in front of Mouton's Division. The deployment of these two Union brigades exceeded slightly the length of Mouton's divisional front. Deployed directly in front of Gray's Louisianians were the 48th Ohio, 19th Kentucky, 96th Ohio, and 83rd Ohio. Polignac's Texans faced the 67th Indiana, 77th Illinois, and 130th Illinois. Emerson's 23rd Wisconsin took a position on the left (south) side of the road facing Walker's Texas division. A powerful array of artillery supported the Union battle line. One section (two guns) of the 6th Missouri Horse Artillery and the six guns of the 2nd Massachusetts Battery occupied a position astride the road on the crest of Honeycutt Hill. The cannon of Company G, 5th U.S. Artillery, together with a section of the Missouri horse artillery closely supported Vance's infantrymen and Lucas' brigade along the right flank of Banks' line. Behind the main Union line the Chicago Mercantile and 1st Indiana batteries unlimbered, the former facing slightly toward the west and the latter toward the north.[25]

Thus far, Richard Taylor had refrained from bringing on a large scale engagement until he could learn whether or not Kirby Smith wanted him to directly engage Banks. By late afternoon, with still no word from his superior, Taylor decided to risk a battle rather than retreat any further in the face of a powerful enemy. About 4:00 p.m. in the afternoon, Mouton received orders to

---

23 Presentation by Judge Felix P. Poche, February 12, 1895, Louisiana Historical Association Collection, Manuscripts Department, Special Collections Division, Tulane University Library.

24   Colonel Joseph Vance's brigade consisted of the 130th Illinois, and the 48th, 83rd, and 96th Ohio regiments. *OR* 34, pt. 1, p. 169.

25   Ibid., pp. 257, 266, 291, 451. Brig. Gen. Thomas E. G. Ransom claims Landram took 2,413 infantry into the fighting at Mansfield. Ibid., pp. 169, 266.

increase the number of his skirmishers and move against the enemy. After Mouton directed Colonel Gray to send his skirmishers forward into the field, he yelled to his old brigade, "Throw down that fence, my boys, and charge across that field and drive the enemy away." The Louisianians, eager for battle, gave a shout and poured over the broken wooden rails.[26]

Prior to the charge, Mouton's officers had agreed that most of them would remain mounted during any attack—an unwise decision that would prove fatal to many of them. The ease with which these brave officers were killed was commented on by one Union soldier, who wrote after the war, "Their field-officers being mounted, [they] were picked off as fast as they came in range."[27] As the Louisianians swept into the open field and easily drove the enemy skirmishers back upon their main line, the Federals poured forth a heavy fire of musketry and artillery into Mouton's charging masses. One Confederate recorded his recollections of this fire in his diary, noting, "The balls and grape shot crashing about us whistled terribly and plowed into the ground and beat our soldiers down even as a storm tears down the trees of a forest." The soldier's memory was indeed accurate. Unfortunately for the Louisianians, they moved out to the attack before the rest of Taylor's army. The result was a ragged, uncoordinated Confederate attack that would cause the Louisianians to suffer the heaviest casualties of the day.[28]

After the attack began, the exact sequence of events becomes confused and is difficult to unwind. The heavy Union fire caused the Louisianians to waver a bit as they crossed the field. Seeing this, Col. James Beard of the Crescent Regiment took his regimental flag from its bearer and urged his men onward. Federal bullets killed him. The Crescent Regiment's lieutenant colonel, Franklin H. Clack, had already fallen mortally wounded earlier in the assault. In an attempt to gain control of the situation, Major Mercer Canfield seized the regimental banner and carried it forward until he too was killed. Colonel Gray noticed the hesitation in the Crescent Regiment and sent his brigade inspector, Lt. Arthur H. Martin, to urge the men onward. Like the others before him, Martin

26   Bergeron, *Reminiscences of Uncle Silas*, pp. 156-157; Bearss, ed., *A Louisiana Confederate*, pp. 105-106.

27   John A. Bering and Thomas Montgomery, *History of the Forty-Eighth Ohio Vet. Vol Inf.* (Hillsboro, 1880), p. 132.

28   Bearss, ed., *A Louisiana Confederate*, p. 107

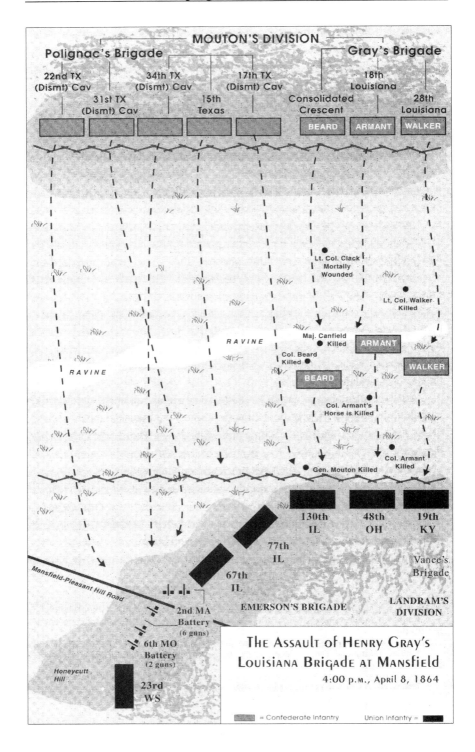

MOUTON'S DIVISION

Polignac's Brigade

22nd TX (Dismt) Cav · 31st TX (Dismt) Cav · 34th TX (Dismt) Cav · 15th Texas · 17th TX (Dismt) Cav

Gray's Brigade

Consolidated Crescent · 18th Louisiana · 28th Louisiana

BEARD · ARMANT · WALKER

Lt. Col. Clack Mortally Wounded

Lt. Col. Walker Killed

RAVINE

Maj. Canfield Killed

ARMANT

Col. Beard Killed

WALKER

RAVINE

BEARD

Col. Armant's Horse is Killed

Col. Armant Killed

Gen. Mouton Killed

130th IL · 48th OH · 19th KY

77th IL

Vance's Brigade

67th IL

Mansfield-Pleasant Hill Road

2nd MA Battery (6 guns)

EMERSON'S BRIGADE

LANDRAM'S DIVISION

6th MO Battery (2 guns)

Honeycutt Hill

23rd WS

THE Assault of Henry Gray's Louisiana Brigade at Mansfield
4:00 p.m., April 8, 1864

= Confederate Infantry   Union Infantry =

merely managed to take up the regiment's flag and order the men to charge before falling mortally wounded.[29]

Soon after Lieutenant Martin fell under the colors of the Consolidated Crescent, Company A's Capt. Seth R. Field picked up his regiment's deadly banner and pushed toward the blazing Union line. Just hours before, as the army marched through Mansfield on its way to Moss Plantation, Field had bid his wife and baby goodbye and hurriedly told them "God bless you." The flag claimed another victim when the young father fell to the ground, his body riddled with Union lead. In all, seven men fell carrying the Crescent Regiment's colors at Mansfield. One observer noted that it seemed as if "entire platoons [of the regiment] fell at every discharge of the enemy's guns."[30]

The fighting at Mansfield is filled with personal vignettes of bravery and sadness. As the Louisianians crossed a ravine running through the field, Mouton ordered his soldiers to drop to the ground for a few moments to catch their breath and reorganize. One officer of the Crescent Regiment, Capt. William C. Claiborne, Jr., a great grandson of Louisiana's first governor, refused the order. Despite attempts by his men to get him to take cover, which included pulling on his coattails to get him to lie down, Claiborne said he preferred to die standing up. Oddly enough, despite his exposure Claiborne was the only captain in the entire regiment to pass through the battle unscathed. Every other captain was killed or wounded. While Claiborne was making his lonely stand above the ravine, an officer in Company B noticed his 1st sergeant, Benjamin D. Wall of Clinton, Louisiana, reading a book while the conflict raged around them. When the officer inquired what he was doing, Wall replied calmly, "I am reading my Bible; I expect to be killed in a few moments." His battlefield prophesy was fulfilled a short time later when an enemy bullet ended his life.[31]

After the brief halt in the ravine, the Louisianians renewed their attack upon Landram's line. One Confederate veteran who witnessed the charge remembered long after the event how the Federal fire caused the Southern line to waver and bend "like a broken reed." Continuing his colorful account, the soldier

---

29   Bergeron, ed., *Reminiscences of Uncle Silas*, p. 157; Gray to Surget, Apr. -, 1864.

30   Unidentified article, "Last of the Mohicans," Mansfield State Commemorative Area Museum; Hewitt, "The Battle of Mansfield," p. 173; *Houston Daily Telegraph*, April -, 1864, quoted in *New Orleans Times*, May 4,1864.

31   Frank L. Richardson, "The Mansfield Campaign," typescript at the Mansfield State Commemorative Area Museum; Bartlett, Military Record of Louisiana, "The Army of the West," p. 6.

recalled that Mouton rode in front of the men and "rallied the boys and straightened that line and made it like the 'Rock of Ages. . . ."[32]

Like her sister regiment on the other end of Gray's line, the 28th Louisiana—stationed on the left of Gray's brigade front—was also having a difficult time against the intense Union fire. Like the unfortunate members of the Crescent Regiment, several of its color bearers were also killed or wounded attempting to cross the field. Sergeant Elie Ganier of the neighboring 18th Louisiana picked up the 28th's flag as it lay on the ground and called upon that regiment to follow him, but an enemy bullet hit him near the knee and disabled him. Major Wilbur F. Blackman, formerly of the 28th and now Mouton's adjutant, grasped his old unit's colors and rode toward the enemy before turning his horse and shouting to his former comrades to rally to their flag. The men responded to the major's exhortations and drove forward, breaking through the enemy's line at the fence. One captured Union soldier reportedly told his captors that no fewer than 200 shots had been fired at Blackman from a distance of less than 50 yards. Despite the close proximity of the warring sides, the gallant officer was not hit.[33]

Captain Arthur W. Hyatt of New Orleans led Company D, 18th Louisiana, into the attack from the center of Gray's line. Hyatt referred to the attack in his diary as "one of the most terrible charges of the war." As he and his men crossed the field, an enemy bullet tore through his left thigh and took him out of action. During the Battle of Shiloh on April 7, 1862, almost exactly two years before the fighting at Mansfield, Hyatt had received a similar wound in his right leg. The only other officer in Hyatt's company present at Mansfield, Lt. Felix E. Nunez, also fell with severe wounds in both legs and his back. Lieutenant Nunez was not as fortunate as his captain. Doctors amputated Nunez's left leg above the knee on May 15, but he failed to rally and died four days later. Of the forty-two men in Hyatt's company who participated in the charge, twenty-nine of them, or 72%, were killed or wounded.[34]

Casualties among Gray's high-ranking officers continued to mount as the Confederates staggered toward the Union line. At some point during the charge across the field, Colonel Armant of the 18th Louisiana was killed. After the

---

32 *Shreveport Times*, April 26, 1925.

33 Bearss, ed., *A Louisiana Confederate*, p. 157; Bergeron, ed., *Reminiscences of Uncle Silas*, p. 107; Bartlett, *Military Record of Louisiana*, "The Trans-Mississippi," p. 62.

34 Hyatt Diary, April 8, 9, May 15, 19, 1864.

gallant colonel's horse was shot from beneath him, he bravely continued to lead his men on foot. When he saw his regimental flag bearer killed, Armant rushed forward and grabbed the colors. His courageous act drew a shower of bullets that struck him down. One officer recalled that when last seen alive, Armant was lying on the ground trying to hold up the flag, encouraging his men forward. After the war, Armant's former quartermaster, Maj. Silas T. Grisamore, recorded the following incident concerning the colonel. According to Grisamore, on the night before the battle Armant told him that he owed another officer money. Armant requested that if he fell in battle, the money be paid from back salary due him. "His looks and language impressed me deeply," noted the major, "and the idea that he had a presentiment of his fate was firmly fixed in my mind."[35]

During the assault of Mouton's Division, Lt. J. E. Sliger of Company B, 28th Louisiana, captured a Federal cavalryman who was attempting to hide in the field. After appropriating his carbine and ammunition, Sliger moved forward and noticed a mounted Federal battery commander riding behind his guns, which had been causing a great number of casualties in his regiment. Realizing his opportunity, the lieutenant dropped to one knee, took aim with his captured weapon, and fired, knocking the officer from his horse. The battery quickly limbered up and retreated, no doubt disheartened by the death of its commander.[36]

Except for occasional shots like Lieutenant Sliger's and other isolated individuals, the Louisianians did not fire on the Federals as they charged across the field. Instead, they halted within a few yards of the Federal line and delivered a volley of musketry into the enemy soldiers. This coordinated fire, coupled with the impetus of the mass assault, broke Colonel Landram's line and drove the Federals back in a rout. Landram detailed the fighting at Mansfield in his official after-action report: "A general engagement ensued, lasting one hour and a half, which was by far the most desperate [fighting] I ever witnessed. Some parts of

35 Bartlett, Military Record of Louisiana, "The Trans-Mississippi," p. 42; Bergeron, ed., *Reminiscences of Uncle Silas*, pp. 226-227.

36 J. E. Sliger, "How General Taylor Fought the Battle of Mansfield, La.," *Confederate Veteran*, 31 (1923), p. 458. This author has been unable to fully verify Sliger's account of the fallen Federal battery commander. Captain Patrick H. White of the Chicago Mercantile Artillery, which supported the Federal line, was wounded during the battle. Lieutenant George Throop of the same unit received a mortal wound, though one account says he was hit by a shell fragment. Alfred T. Andreas, *History of Chicago, From the Earliest Period to the Present Time*, 3 vols. (Chicago, 1884-1886), vol. 2, pp. 282-287, 299; *Chicago Tribune*, April 21, 1864.

the line were broken after a short but terrific engagement, but in other parts it remained firm and unbroken until the enemy had flanked my whole force and began an attack in the rear. Seeing that the capture of the entire force was inevitable unless I withdrew, I ordered the remainder of the shattered regiments to fall back, which they attempted, but were unable to accomplish with entire success."[37]

The 28th Louisiana took cover behind the fence from which they had just driven the Federals. Unfortunately, the 18th and Crescent Regiments did not follow suit. Both of these wounded units stood to return the fire of the retreating foe and received a last heavy volley of musketry and artillery. One of those soldiers hit along the fence line by this fire was Capt. S. Alexander Poche of the 18th Louisiana, who was struck by an enemy bullet which passed through the upper part of his right thigh, just missing the bone and main artery. Two privates of the 28th Louisiana tried to carry Captain Poche from the field, but one of the men fell wounded during the attempt, and the captain ordered the other private back to his regiment. The wounded Poche lay on the battlefield until sundown, when some of his own men found him and took him to a hospital. Poche's subordinates also did not fare well. His second lieutenant, J. Septime Webre, was severely wounded when his right arm was pierced by a musket ball that shattered the limb so badly surgeons had to amputate it. Poche's third lieutenant, F. M. Ganier, received a slight wound above the knee as the Federals withdrew in panicked confusion.[38]

Just as his regimental commanders had fallen in the fighting, so too did Colonel Gray's own staff suffer the effects of the Federal fire. Adam Beatty of Thibodaux, Louisiana, a volunteer aide for Colonel Gray, was one of those killed beyond the captured fence line in the woods from which the first Union line was driven. Gray, who had a premonition that his friend would be injured in the fighting, had advised Beatty not to go into the upcoming battle. He was trying to think of an excuse to send Beatty to the rear when the attack began, but the old gentleman went out with the troops into the field. As if defying Gray's forewarning, Beatty passed through the initial hail of fire unhurt. As the staffer

---

37 *OR* 34, pt. 1, p. 292; *Houston Daily Telegraph*, April -, 1864, quoted in *New Orleans Times*, May 4,1864; Bearss, ed., *A Louisiana Confederate*, p. 107.

38 Poche, "Battle of Mansfield"; Application of Elie Ganier, Act 96 of 1884, State Land Office Records, Louisiana State Archives; Application of J. S. Webre, Act 116 of 1886. Ibid.

advanced through the woods, however, an enemy ball hit him in the stomach. He died the next morning.[39]

Another member of Gray's staff was wounded in the attack. John L. Lewis of New Orleans, a former commander of the state militia, had also volunteered to serve Gary as an aide. Major Grisamore, mentioned above, recalled that even "with his white and flowing locks [Lewis] acted like a youthful cavalier [during the attack]." A Federal minie ball struck the white-maned Lewis on the head and knocked him from his horse. The injury was not serious, however, and Lewis stopped only long enough to bind the wound before rejoining the battle. Gray reported that Lewis "assisted me materially, conducting himself with all the ardor and fire of youth, and was conspicuous in the whole field."[40]

Although the Southern officer corps suffered heavily in killed and wounded, the most severe loss of the day was the death of Taylor's division commander, Brig. Gen. Alfred Mouton. Although surviving accounts of his death vary in detail, the accounts agree on the basic elements of his untimely demise. The Confederates had just succeeded in breaking the enemy line and were rounding up prisoners and captured enemy equipment when Mouton rode upon a group of Federals numbering from 15-35 men. The Federals threw down their weapons and surrendered to him. At this point Mouton turned to make sure that approaching Confederate soldiers did not accidentally shoot at the prisoners. Taking advantage of their opportunity, five Federals stooped down and retrieved their rifled-muskets when they saw that Mouton was alone and well ahead of his men. All five soldiers fired at the mounted officer. As the Cajun general fell from his saddle, Confederates who had witnessed the treachery rushed in and killed the entire group of Federals before their officers could restrain them.[41]

Richard Taylor later noted that of all the deaths that day, Mouton's grieved him the most. "Of the Louisianians fallen, most were acquaintances, many had been neighbors and friends; and they were gone. Above all, the death of gallant Mouton affected me. He had joined me soon after I reached western Louisiana, and had ever proved faithful to duty. Modest, unselfish, and patriotic, he showed

---

39   Bergeron, ed., *Reminiscences of Uncle Silas*, p. 158; Bearss, ed., *A Louisiana Confederate*, p. 107.

40   Bergeron, ed., *Reminiscences of Uncle Silas*, p. 159; Bearss, ed., *A Louisiana Confederate*, p. 107; Gray to Surget, April –, 1864.

41   Bergeron, ed., *Reminiscences of Uncle Silas*, pp. 214-215; Bearss, ed., *A Louisiana Confederate*, p. 107; Bartlett, *Military Record of Louisiana*, "The Trans-Mississippi," p. 42; William Arceneaux, *Acadian General: Alfred Mouton and the Civil War* (Lafayette, 1981), p. 132.

best in action, always leading his men. I thought of his wife and children, and of his father, Governor Mouton, whose noble character I have attempted to portray." For Taylor, the loss of the gallant Mouton was irreplaceable.[42]

The infantry of John George Walker's Texas division, aligned on the west side of the Pleasant Hill Road, did not become engaged until after Mouton's division had crushed the Federal line facing it. By the time the Texans charged from their position in the woods across the open space in front of Honeycutt Hill, only the dismounted men of Dudley's brigade, the 67th Indiana, and the 23rd Wisconsin were left to oppose the assault. As the Texans moved forward, two regiments of Texas cavalry under Brig. Gen. Hamilton P. Bee swept around the Union left flank. The cavalry thrust threatened to engulf the Federals. With Bee on the flank and the Texans in front, the enemy quickly fell back in a rout. Several cannon of the 2nd Massachusetts Battery fell into the hands of the Texans, who turned them to fire on the retreating Federals. Walker's victorious soldiers began sending hundreds of captured Union soldiers toward the rear.[43]

Although they routed one Federal division (Landram's), the victorious Confederates soon found another division deployed in line of battle across their front. This second line consisted of the two brigades from Brig. Gen. Robert A. Cameron's Third Division, XIII Corps. Cameron's 1,293 men had reached this position about 4:15 p.m., just minutes after Mouton's attack broke across the front of Banks' vanguard. Cameron placed his 2nd Brigade on the left of the road just above Sabine Cross Roads. His 1st Brigade formed its lines on the right side of the road.[44]

The Louisianians, who struck Cameron's position first, again wavered a bit as they waded through the woods through heavy Union musketry. Lieutenant Edwin C. Kidd of the 28th Louisiana seized his regiment's colors and carried them toward the enemy, calling upon the men to follow him. Cameron later reported that his small force held its position for nearly an hour against the repeated Confederate onslaughts. The renewed attack by Gray's brigade,

---

42   Taylor, *Destruction and Reconstruction*, p. 198.

43   J. P. Blessington, *The Campaigns of Walker's Texas Division* (Austin, 1968), pp. 183-187; T. R. Bonner, "Sketches of the Campaign of 1864," *The Land We Love*, Vol. V (I 868), pp. 460-463.

44   Lieutenant Colonel Aaron M. Flory's 1st Brigade had only two regiments, the 46th Indiana and the 29th Wisconsin. Colonel William H. Raynor's 2nd Brigade consisted of the 24th and 28th Iowa regiments, and the 56th Ohio. *OR* 34, pt. 1, p. 169.

strengthened by Polignac's brigade and Walker's Texans, eventually flanked and routed this second Federal line.[45]

Late in the day, the Confederates attacked yet a third position held by another portion of Banks' army. About 5,000 men of Brig. Gen. William H. Emory's First Division, XIX Corps, had formed a line on the high ground south of Chatman's Bayou, about three miles southeast of the main battlefield. The Confederates drove in Emory's skirmishers and boldly charged his main line. This initial assault was driven back with heavy losses. Polignac—who had assumed command of Mouton's Division after that officer was killed during the first stage of the battle— led his battered pair of brigades in a failed attempt to outflank the Federals on their right. Similar efforts against the Union left flank were also pushed back. Nightfall finally brought an end to the fighting, and the exhausted and badly bloodied Confederates allowed the enemy to continue their retreat unmolested. The deep Southern penetration succeeded in gaining access to the badly-needed water available in the Chatman Bayou.[46]

Richard Taylor's army had won a smashing victory at Mansfield. Federal losses numbered 113 men killed, 581 wounded, and 1,541 captured or missing out of the approximately 7,000 engaged. Twenty pieces of artillery, 200 wagons loaded with supplies, and thousands of small arms fell into Confederate hands. Tactically, Taylor's attack at Mansfield met and defeated in detail two of Banks' infantry divisions and three of his cavalry brigades. The battle proved to be the strategic turning point of the campaign as well. The political general's battered army retreated after its drubbing at Mansfield, and Banks' confidence was greatly shaken by the sharp defeat. In practical terms, Taylor's army gained some much needed artillery and small arms, as well as other supplies found in the captured Union wagon train.[47]

The cost of Taylor's success, however, was heavy. Confederate losses totaled nearly 1,000 men. Because the Louisiana brigade had borne the brunt of the fighting, its losses were very high. Gray's Brigade suffered almost 400

45 Ibid., p. 273; Bartlett, *Military Record of Louisiana*, "The Trans-Mississippi," p. 62; Bearss, ed., *A Louisiana Confederate*, p. 107. Unfortunately, Confederate accounts do not provide the level of detail on this and subsequent phases of the battle available on the initial assault against Banks' army. Perhaps the attack made such an impression on their minds that the confused fighting that followed seemed anti-climactic. Unfortunately, available Federal battle reports do not provide any substantive descriptions of the latter stages of the fighting.

46 *OR* 34, pt. 1, pp. 260, 392, 417, 42 1.

47 Ibid., pp. 263-264, 391-392, 452, 527.

casualties (about 40% Of its effective strength) in the late afternoon fighting, with most of these coming from the Consolidated Crescent Regiment. Colonel Beard's contingent, which had advanced on the right flank of the brigade, lost 57 men killed and 134 wounded, including Col. James Beard, Lt. Col. Franklin H. Clack, Maj. Mercer Canfield, Capt. Seth Field, Capt. Charles D. Moore, Capt. William M. Fuller, and Lt. C. M. Horton, all killed or mortally wounded. The 18th Louisiana, which had held the center of Gray's Brigade, lost 19 men killed and 75 wounded, including Col. Leopold L. Armant, Capt. John T. Lavery, and Lt. Felix E. Nunez, all of whom were killed or mortally wounded. Other officer casualties included Capt. S. Alexander Poche, Capt. Arthur W. Hyatt, Lt. Thomas D. Melville, Lt. J. Septime Webre, Lt. Louis Becnel, and Lt. F. M. Ganier, all wounded. No exact figures exist for the casualties of the brigade's left-most regiment, the 28th Louisiana. Given its similar performance during the fighting and its adjacent deployment on the left of the 18th Louisiana, it is logical to conclude that the 28th suffered similar losses. As noted with each regiment above, Gray's officer corps was effectively wiped out. Every field officer present in the brigade at Mansfield was killed or mortally wounded. At least seventeen officers of the 18th and Crescent regiments fell dead or wounded, several suffering more than one wound in the process.[48]

Even though he went into the fighting mounted and spent most of the battle in the forefront of his men, Gray somehow escaped injury. Although diminutive in stature, the Louisiana colonel rode a large horse named Cesar into the battle, prompting many of men to humorously refer to him as a "baby on a monument." After the battle, one of Gray's staff officers lucky enough to have survived the fighting asked him whether he thought the Yankees would get him during the battle. Gray replied that his only fear was that they might shoot Cesar.[49]

Most historical documents relate accounts about officers, but the common soldiers unfortunately have little written about them. Private Charles J. Barker of Company G, 18th Louisiana, went through a horrible experience at Mansfield. During the charge of Gray's Brigade, a Minie ball struck him in the right leg, breaking both of the lower bones in that limb. Through someone's oversight,

---

48 Bearss. ed., *A Louisiana Confederate*, p. 107; Bartlett, *Military Record of Louisiana*, "Army of the West," p. 6; List of casualties dated May 30, 1864, signed by Lieut. James B. Rosser, Hyatt Papers; *Shreveport Semi-Weekly News*, May 3, 1864. The lack of records makes it impossible to determine the exact strength of Gray's brigade (or of its individual regiments) at the time of the battle. Mouton's division probably numbered no more than 2,200 men on April 8,1864.

49 Bergeron, ed., *Reminiscences of Uncle Silas*, p. 2 10.

those who combed the field for dead and wounded soldiers after the battle did not immediately find the wounded private, and he lay where he fell for three days without medical attention. When he was finally located and taken to one of the improvised hospitals in town, he had to "lay on the floor eight days before the surgeons attended to his case." This long delay resulted in Barker having his leg amputated about a month later.[50]

Although Barker's battlefield drama is moving, there is another, more touching episode involving another common soldier at Mansfield. Private Stephen D. Lord, Company G, Consolidated Crescent Regiment, owned a farm several miles south of the battlefield. Prior to the fighting, he managed a brief visit to his wife as the army marched from Pleasant Hill to Mansfield. While in camp on April 6, another soldier accidentally discharged his weapon. The ball hit Lord in the head and cut his skin to the bone. Only his thick hat prevented him from receiving serious injury or death. Lord paused for a moment the following day to write a letter to his wife explaining the details of the incident. He expressed concern about soldiers from both armies confiscating the little bit of meat and corn his wife had left. The private never learned how his wife fared with two large armies in close proximity, for he was killed during the battle on April 8. His wife traveled to Mansfield the day after the battle and claimed his body, burying it in a nearby cemetery.[51]

Most of the houses in Mansfield were converted into hospitals following the battle. Diarist Capt. Felix Pierre Poche visited the town the next day and was sufficiently moved to describe in his diary the sadness he witnessed there: "What a pitiful sight were those hospitals crowded with the wounded, the dying and the dead, friends and enemies side by side, some calling for help, others groaning in pain so pitifully that I left with a heavy heart."[52] One of those who tended the wounded was the recently-widowed wife of Capt. Seth R. Field of the Crescent

50 Ibid., p. 158; John B. Dimitry, "Louisiana," *Confederate Military History*, 12 vols. (Atlanta, 1899), vol. 10, p. 334; Application of Charles J. Barker, Act 96 of 1884, State Land Office Records. Private Barker owed his life to Miss Laura Crosby, a young lady who had him moved from the hospital to her father's house. Barker spent ten months recovering from his wound before his was physically able to return home, where he found his father's property ruined by the war. Dimitry, "Louisiana," pp. 334-335.

51 Stephen D. Lord Letter, April 7, 1864, Mansfield State Commemorative Area Museum. Private Lord's last letter is on public display at the museum.

52 Bearss, ed., *A Louisiana Confederate*, p. 108; Pvt. Julien Rachat to sister, April 12, 1864, a handwritten translation housed at the Mansfield State Commemorative Area Museum.

Regiment. After she recovered her husband's corpse from the battlefield and had it buried, she turned to the work of assisting the injured.[53]

After its defeat at Mansfield, the Union army fell back to Pleasant Hill, where the troops of the XVI Corps had encamped. Taylor's army, reinforced by the recently-arrived infantry from the District of Arkansas, attacked the Federals again on April 9. Although initially successful, the Confederate assault eventually stalled and was forced back with heavy losses. Gray's Louisiana brigade remained in reserve during the Pleasant Hill battle and as a result suffered few casualties. The Federals lost heavily again in this second round of fighting, suffering 152 men killed, 859 wounded, and 495 missing. Taylor's Confederates also suffered heavy casualties, about 1,200 men killed and wounded, and 426 captured.[54] Although the Confederates suffered a tactical defeat at Pleasant Hill, the renewal of the Federal retreat to Grand Ecore during the night of April 9-10 transformed the battle into a strategic victory for Richard Taylor's exuberant army. Taylor's savage assaults on April 8 and 9 convinced Banks that he could not successfully continue the campaign, so he ordered his army to withdraw to Natchitoches.[55]

The Federals remained near Natchitoches for several days before continuing their retreat toward Alexandria. Taylor, thanks to Kirby Smith, pursued Banks with a greatly reduced force. The department commander seized from his subordinate not only the two divisions from the District of Arkansas, but John Walker's three Texas brigades as well. Smith used these pilfered troops in a fruitless pursuit of Steele's Union army, which was retreating toward Little Rock. After the dismantling of his victorious army, Taylor was left with only Polignac's small infantry division and a reorganized cavalry corps under Maj. Gen. John A. Wharton consisting of the divisions of James Major, Hamilton Bee, and William Steele. As would be expected, Taylor's cavalry did most of the skirmishing with the Federals during the ensuing weeks. Banks' army, forced to halt at Alexandria during construction of a dam in the Red River that would allow Porter's fleet to get over the falls near that town, finally moved downriver on May 13. Southern cavalry continued to harass its enemy as Banks marched through Marksville and Mansura. On May 18, the Confederates fought the

---

53   "Last of the Mohicans," Mansfield State Commemorative Area Museum.

54   *OR* 34, pt. 1, pp. 313, 398, 452; Bearss, *A Louisiana Confederate*, p. 106; Gray to Surget, Apr. –, 1864; Taylor, *Destruction and Reconstruction*, p. 206.

55   Johnson, *Red River Campaign*, 154-169.

Union rear guard in a sharp action at Yellow Bayou. Gray's Brigade played a significant role in this battle and lost, according to one account, 40 killed, 31 wounded, and 25 missing. The engagement was strategically inconclusive and both sides lost heavily. The next day all of Banks' army crossed the Atchafalaya River at Simmesport, effectively ending the campaign.[56]

The Red River Campaign represented one of the last major successes for the Confederacy. By defeating Banks along the Red River, Taylor prolonged the war for several months. Since A. J. Smith's men (a two-division veteran detachment from the Army of the Tennessee) could not join William T. Sherman in northern Georgia, Sherman took many thousands of fewer men with him against Gen. Joseph E. Johnston than he had counted upon. The delay in conducting a campaign against the critical port of Mobile, Alabama, permitted the Confederates to heavily reinforce Johnston with troops from Mississippi and Alabama, men which might otherwise have had to defend Mobile. A. J. Smith's detachment and the consequent results that flowed from Taylor's victories hampered Sherman's drive toward Atlanta, his subsequent "March to the Sea," and his final campaign in the Carolinas. A Union victory in the Red River Campaign would certainly have hastened the end of the war.[57]

The Louisiana brigade performed valiantly at Mansfield. Well-disciplined after more than two years of service and inspired by the desire to drive the enemy from their native state, the men endured a galling fire of artillery and musketry before forcing the Federals to retreat. A veteran exaggerated only slightly when he wrote: "The charge of Mouton's Division at Mansfield was certainly a splendid one, and one that was not often excelled in vigor and impetuosity."[58]

*   *   *

Postscript: After the fighting, Taylor recommended Gray for promotion but Kirby Smith declined, writing cryptically, "His habits, I understand, are not good." Taylor persisted and Smith relented on April 15, with the promotion to date from April 8, 1864. Gray left the brigade to fill a seat in Congress later that year. He served one term in the state senate after the war. He died in Louisiana on December 11, 1892.

---

56   Bearss, ed., *A Louisiana Confederate*, pp. 122-23; *OR* 34, pt. 1, pp. 311, 594-595; Taylor, *Destruction and Reconstruction*, p. 232; Johnson, *Red River Campaign*, pp. 221-222, 235, 248-250, 266-276.

57   Johnson, *Red River Campaign*, pp. 278-279.

58   Bergeron, ed., *Reminiscences of Uncle Silas*, p. 159.

Gary D. Joiner & Charles E. Vetter

Union Naval Operations on the Red River, March 12-May 22, 1864

*T*he spring of 1864 Red River Campaign was one of the most important operations waged west of the Mississippi River. Although not as significant militarily as the concurrent campaigns waged in Georgia and Virginia, ultimately it would affect those operations and prolong the war. Without argument, the Red River Campaign ended in the most decisive Confederate victory achieved on Louisiana soil. Although fascinating in all of its complicated aspects, what little has been written on this campaign has tended to focus on the two principal land engagements of the campaign, the battles of Mansfield (Sabine Cross Roads), fought on April 8, and Pleasant Hill, waged the following day. Unfortunately, the naval aspect of the expedition up Red River has been treated as little more than a secondary movement in support of Nathaniel Banks and his land-based army. Only two major works address the campaign from the perspective of the Union navy—the Confederate naval activities have been all but obliterated from consideration—and both of these were penned by Rear Adm. David Dixon Porter, the Union commander of the Mississippi Squadron.[1] As one would expect, in spite of the value of these firsthand accounts, they are biased and at times inaccurate. A close examination of the literature and, perhaps more importantly, the manuscript materials relating to the Red River Expedition, yields a wealth of detail about this long neglected and largely unexplored naval campaign.

The purpose of this essay is to address primarily the naval aspects of the Union efforts to capture Shreveport, Louisiana, whose fall would have effectively removed a large portion of the Confederate Trans-Mississippi from the war. This article is limited to the period between the entry of the Union fleet

---

1   David D. Porter, *The Naval History of the Civil War* (Secaucus, 1984), and Porter, *Incidents and Anecdotes of the Civil War* (New York, 1885).

into Red River at the end of February 1864, and its exit into the Mississippi River almost three months later.

General-in-Chief Winfield Scott, hero of the War with Mexico and in 1860 the most venerated soldier of the United States army, set the course which would ultimately win the war for the North. His strategy was dubbed by the press as the "Anaconda Plan," named for the large Amazon basin reptile that kills its prey by coiling around its victim, suffocating it while crushing its vital organs. Under Scott's conception of the plan, the Union would attempt the same technique to destroy its Southern foe. Although in theory the concept was simple enough, its application proved much more difficult. The plan called for Northern naval forces to blockade the Southern coastline while occupying the South's major rivers; Union armies would deny control of the land to the Southern military and government. The North would coil around the Confederacy, suffocate it, and crush its ability to carry on the war.

The conflict quickly divided into three major theaters of operation: the Virginia Theater east of the Appalachian Mountains; the Western Theater west of the Appalachians and east of the Mississippi River; and the Trans-Mississippi area of operations, the vast expanse of territory west of that river. The lengthy and meandering Southern coastline made the Union blockade ineffective during the early years. As the war dragged on, its effectiveness in bottling up the South's major ports increased. The acquisition of territory proved more difficult and required not only talented leadership in the field, but an awareness of the importance of rivers as highways of commerce, communication and strategic mobility.

Both sides recognized the importance of the inland waterways even before the war began, and a large portion of the history of the Civil War—especially in the Western and Trans-Mississippi Theaters—chronicles the struggle to control these vital waterways. Both antagonists knew that control of the Mississippi River was the key to the war in the West. The Mississippi was the best north-south route in the Confederacy, in addition to being the eastern terminus for goods shipped from the Trans-Mississippi Department (west of the river) and up from Mexico. If the North could effectively control the Mississippi, the South would be cleaved in two large chunks.

If the Mississippi was the key to the war in the West, Vicksburg was the lock that opened the door on the Union strategy for victory in the Mississippi River Valley. The capture of Vicksburg, the greatest Confederate stronghold on the river, occupied the Union armies in the West from the latter part of 1862 until its fall on July 4, 1863. Soon after, Port Hudson, another river stronghold in southern Louisiana, surrendered and the "Father of Waters flowed unvexed to the Sea."[2] The double defeats at Vicksburg and Port Hudson all but completely severed the Confederacy west of the Mississippi River from the remainder of the South. Texas, southern Arkansas, north and central Louisiana, and half of the Indian Territory were still in Confederate hands west of the river. The Union held north and central Arkansas, New Orleans, Baton Rouge, and the bayou country of southern Louisiana.

Federally-controlled areas in Louisiana were primarily flat prairie or marshy lands accessible via rivers and bayous or by the few roads that snaked inland away from the rivers. The Confederates held the Red River Valley and the hill country in the north and central portion of the state. They also controlled territory in southern Arkansas and east Texas. These areas were either flat cotton producing stream valleys or vast tracts of pine forests that grew thick and extended all across the region. In the hill country, few roads cut through these forests and the pines encroached up to the road beds. Wresting these lands from the Confederates would be a major and difficult task.

Union origins of the Red River expedition of 1864 are somewhat obscure, especially because no one associated with Northern arms wanted to take credit for suggesting or planning it following its disastrous outcome. Although many of the participants left reports, letters, and diaries recording the events which transpired along the Red River, many aspects of its genesis are more difficult to precisely identify than they should be. Thankfully, historians have heaped enough blame on the principal Union participants to cast some light on the subject.

It appears the idea for the campaign originated in 1861 and was motivated by both political and military factors. A possible Confederate attack on Mexico had to be forestalled, occupation of Matamoros by European powers had to be prevented, Confederate trade with Mexico had to be disrupted, and Texas settlers and Unionists needed to be protected and/or rescued from the Secessionists. Every early Union attempt to successfully invade Texas had failed, and by 1862, when Maj. Gen. Nathaniel P. Banks replaced Maj. Gen. Benjamin F. Butler as commander of the Union Department of the Gulf, it was Banks' understanding that he was to continue with efforts to invade the Lone Star state.[3] However, the Lincoln administration's policy regarding the acquisition of Texas soil shifted

---

2   Henry Steele Commager, ed., *The Blue and the Grey: The Story of the Civil War as Told by the Participants*, 2 vols. (Indianapolis, 1950), vol. 2, p. 677.

3   The War of the Rebellion: *The Official Records of the Union and Confederate Armies*, 128 vols. (Washington, D.C., 1890-1901), series 1, vol. 25, pp. 590. Hereinafter cited as *OR*. All references are to series I unless otherwise noted.

soon after Banks took command. Instead of incursions into Texas, Banks was to concentrate his efforts on helping to wrest the Mississippi River from Confederate control. General-in-Chief Henry Halleck wrote Banks that Lincoln "regards the opening of the Mississippi River as the first and most important of all our military and naval operations, and it is hoped you will not lose a moment in accomplishing it." Once this had been accomplished, other operations might be considered, such as an expedition up Red River to release the cotton and sugar of that area and to establish a base for an advance on Texas. In line with his orders, Banks immediately began preparations for the operation that, following the fall of Vicksburg, ultimately led to the surrender of the Confederate bastion at Port Hudson.[4]

With the Mississippi free of Confederate control, talk was renewed of an invasion of Texas via Louisiana's Red River. On July 29, 1863, President Lincoln wrote to Secretary of War Edwin M. Stanton: "Can we not renew the effort to organize a force to go to Western Texas?"[5] The following week on August 5, Lincoln wrote Major General Banks that "recent events in Mexico, I think, render early action in Texas more important than ever."[6] Halleck had been thinking along the same lines as early as July 24, when he had written Banks that he considered an attack on Texas to be of utmost importance, and that "every preparation should be made for an expedition into Texas."[7]

The plan was opposed by both Maj. Gen. Ulysses S. Grant, architect of the successful Vicksburg operation, and Nathaniel Banks, the captor of Port Hudson. They believed instead that the next Union objective should be Mobile, Alabama, an important seaport and rail connection. Grant feared the Texas expedition would siphon off badly needed troops that could be better used in the spring campaigns east of the Mississippi River. Although Banks concurred with Grant's assessment, Halleck was determined to move into Texas before attempting to capture Mobile. Not only had Halleck made up his mind to have Banks move on Texas—a plan Halleck had been sitting on since November, 1862—he had also determined the route that should be taken. In his order assigning Banks as commander of the Department of the Gulf, Halleck recommended that a thrust along the meandering Red River would be the most effective route to Shreveport and Texas. As Banks would later write, "That

4 Ibid.

5 *OR* 26, pt. 1, p. 559.

6 Ibid., p. 384.

7 Ibid., p. 653.

Major General Nathaniel Banks

movement had always been pressed upon me by General Halleck before I left Washington to assume command of that department."[8]

With the fall of Vicksburg and Port Hudson, Halleck renewed his efforts for a drive into Texas. On August 10, 1863, he wrote: "In my opinion, neither Indianola nor Galveston is the proper point of attack. If it be necessary, as urged by Mr. [Secretary of State William H.] Seward, that the flag be restored to some one point in Texas, that can be best and most safely effected by a combined military and naval movement up Red River to Alexandria, Natchitoches, or Shreveport, and the military occupation of Northern Texas."[9]

Banks was uneasy about this plan and raised numerous logistical objections to the Red River route.[10] Instead of moving up Red River, Banks believed the

---

8   The Report of the Joint Committee on the Conduct of the War, 38th Congress, 2nd session, vol. 2, p. 5. Hereinafter cited as Joint Committee on the Conduct of the War.

9   *OR* 26, pt, 1, p. 673.

10 Ibid., pp. 888-890.

most effective way to invade Texas was an amphibious approach on the coast near Sabine Pass, followed by a movement on Galveston and other points on the coast.[11] From August to December, 1863, Banks made a number of attempts to carry out this plan with but minor success.[12] Halleck was not pleased with the results and in January 1864 wrote Banks: "Generals [William T.] Sherman and [Frederick] Steele agree with me in opinion that the Red River is the shortest and best line of defense for Louisiana and Arkansas and as a base of operations against Texas." Banks eventually muted his opposition to the plan.[13]

Nathaniel P. Banks was appointed commander of the Department of the Gulf in large part because of pressure placed on President Lincoln by New England manufacturers, who desired a change in the confrontational policy of Benjamin Butler. In addition, they urged the immediate occupation of Texas. Their motives were not purely patriotic. The occupation of Texas (and the conquest of Louisiana's Red River Valley) would make it easier for New England's factories to obtain large supplies of cotton and other staples—and Banks appeared to be the perfect choice for opening these areas. He was the son of a Waltham, Massachusetts, cotton factory superintendent who taught him the value of this economic miracle fiber. Banks displayed an aptitude for public life, served as a member of the state bar, and eventually became a state legislator. He served as Speaker of the House of Massachusetts, United States congressman, and prior to the outbreak of the war, as governor of the Commonwealth of Massachusetts. Banks wielded a substantial amount of clout as a result of his political career and had established formidable ties to the financial world. In addition, he had become a very successful entrepreneur.

Though utterly without military experience except with the state militia, in May 1861 Banks was appointed major general of volunteers and assigned command of the V Corps of the Army of the Potomac. Once in uniform, the newly commissioned officer quickly found himself in an important position in the Shenandoah Valley. Unfortunately for Banks and the Union, his opponent was Maj. Gen. Thomas J. "Stonewall" Jackson, who soon exposed Banks' deficiencies as a field commander. After his thrashing in the Valley, Banks

---

11 Maj. Gen. N. P. Banks to General-in-Chief H. W. Halleck, August 26,1863, ibid., pp. 696-697.

12 Frank Welcher, *The Union Army, 1861-1865, Organization and Operations, Volume 2: The Western Theater* (Bloomington, 1993), pp. 318-319, for brief discussions of these efforts.

13 Ibid., 34, pt. 2, p. 15.

commanded the vanguard of Maj. Gen. John Pope's Army of Virginia against his nemesis Jackson in the August 9, 1862, Battle of Cedar Mountain, where the fortuitous arrival of reinforcements saved his command. Afterward, he found himself in command of the defenses of Washington, D.C., and from there was sent to the Department of the Gulf, where he earned laurels capturing Port Hudson.

For a number of years Banks had his eyes on the Republican nomination for president. The Civil War offered him the unique opportunity to build a military career that would catapult him into the White House in 1864. This desire meant that, like it or not, he had to cooperate with Henry Halleck. On January 23, 1864, Banks, succumbing to politics and cotton, wrote to the general-in-chief, "I concur in your opinion, and with Generals Sherman and Steele, that the Red River is the shortest and best line of defense for Louisiana and Arkansas, and as a base of operations against Texas, but it would be too much for General Steele or myself to undertake separately. With our united forces and the assistance of General Sherman the success of movements on that line will be certain and important. I shall most cordially co-operate with them in executing your order."[14]

After throwing his support behind Halleck's plan, Banks opened a correspondence with Maj. Gen. Frederick Steele, commander of the Department of Arkansas, Sherman, and Porter, for the purpose of developing a coordinated plan of action. Major General William T. Sherman, who had played a major role in the Vicksburg Campaign, began to show increased interest in the Red River venture. Although in the middle of his Meridian expedition in Mississippi, he had indicated to both Steele and Grant his desire to participate in a move against Shreveport. He had previously expressed a similar desire to Admiral Porter.[15] Sherman's interest probably resulted from his past ties with Louisiana, particularly the Red River valley. He had been the superintendent of the Louisiana Seminary of Learning and Military Academy in Pineville, Louisiana, just prior to the war. His brief tenure as an educator was a pleasant one and the chances were good that had the war not broken out and had Louisiana not seceded, he would have made Louisiana his long-term domicile. Pineville is on

14 *OR* 34, pt. 2, p. 133.

15 Porter, *Naval History*, p. 494; *OR* 32, pt. 2, pp. 169, 189-190, 201-202, 270-271. More on Sherman's largely-ignored Meridian Campaign can be found in Margie Riddle Bearss, *Sherman's Forgotten Campaign: The Meridian Expedition* (Jackson, 1987), the only full-length treatment of this period of the war in Mississippi.

Red River adjacent to the city of Alexandria, and only 150 miles from Shreveport. Sherman knew the area and could assist in making the expedition a success. But he also knew it would be a difficult expedition. Perhaps better than any Union officer involved in the move against Shreveport, he was aware of the unpredictability and vagaries of Red River. Grant, Sherman's immediate superior, was unenthusiastic about the venture, but his close friendship with Sherman caused him to reluctantly give his consent to the move. Unlike Halleck, Grant did not think an expedition against Mobile, Alabama, should be delayed at the expense of the time and cost—in terms of both borrowed manpower and treasure—it would take to capture Shreveport. He told Sherman as much, and that he feared any troops sent "will be permanently lost from his command."[16]

Returning to Vicksburg from his Meridian expedition and having received permission from Grant, Sherman traveled down the Mississippi to New Orleans to discuss the maneuver with Banks. In actuality Sherman headed to the Crescent City believing he would command the expedition up the Red, a fact he mentioned in a letter to his wife. Not only did he want the command but, according to Sherman, Grant also wanted him to lead the campaign.[17]

Upon arriving in New Orleans, Sherman learned that Halleck had selected Banks as the field commander and that Maj. Gen. John A. McClernand, Sherman and Grant's old political enemy from the Vicksburg Campaign, might be a part of the expedition. With this knowledge in hand, Sherman, himself an astute politician, wisely decided he would not take part in a campaign led by a politically-talented but militarily inept commander. In addition, he had no desire to be anywhere near McClernand. Sherman gracefully—he was capable of being graceful when the situation required—backed out of the expedition. He did agree, however, to send 10,000 men up Red River to act in concert with Admiral Porter and his fleet. He dictated two major terms regarding their use, however: his men would not advance further than Shreveport, and that they be returned to his command on or about April 15, 1864.[18] Sherman eventually selected Brig. Gen. Andrew J. Smith's veteran infantry divisions for the assignment with Banks, knowing that Smith and his men would cooperate fully with the Navy "in the most energetic manner." He assured Banks that Porter had already decided to

---

16   Ibid., pp. 224-225.

17   Mark DeWolfe Howe, ed, *Home Letters of General Sherman* (New York, 1909), pp. 286-287.

18   *OR* 34, pt. 2, pp. 494, 496.

participate in the campaign and would provide "every ironclad vessel in the fleet."[19]

Having completed his business, Sherman made ready to return to the more politically safe atmosphere of Vicksburg. Banks urged him to remain a few days to participate in the inauguration ceremonies of Michael Hahn, the newly-elected Union Governor of Louisiana. Sherman, upon his arrival in New Orleans, had already witnessed the preparations being made for this event and noticed that most of it was being supervised by Banks himself. He wisely concluded that Banks would not devote time to military affairs until after the inauguration, something that disturbed him greatly. He refused the general's invitation, stating later in his memoirs that he "regarded all such ceremonies as out of place at a time when it seemed to me every hour and minute were due to the war."[20] After completing his brief military conference with Banks, he departed for Vicksburg, thereby severing his relationship with the Red River expedition.

Thus as it turned out, Nathaniel Banks had agreed, albeit reluctantly, to accept Halleck's idea of grand strategy by commanding a thrust up Red River. Grant, hesitant about the prospects of the expedition and its effect on other campaigns, had given permission for Sherman to send 10,000 of his men to Louisiana to assist Banks. The naval segment of the move was nailed down when Porter guaranteed the complete cooperation of his fleet. The only remaining component to complete the plans for an invasion up Red River to Shreveport, and eventually Texas, was the second prong in Halleck's strategy, the southern approach from Arkansas.

Despite Halleck's best efforts, excitement for the campaign, especially from the Arkansas wing commander, proved less than enthusiastic. Major General Frederick Steele, a New York native, attended West Point and graduated with the same class as Ulysses S. Grant in 1843. After routine garrison duty in New York and Michigan, he fought with distinction in the Mexican War, winning brevets of first lieutenant and captain. His first important action during the Civil War was as a commander of a battalion of Regulars at Wilson's Creek. On September 23, 1861, he was appointed colonel of the 8th Iowa Volunteers and was promoted to brigadier general on January 29, 1862. He was promoted to major general after

---

19 Porter, *Naval History*, p. 495; U.S. War Department, *Official Records of the Union and Confederate Navies in the War of the Rebellion*, 31 vols. (Washington, D.C., 1895-1929), series 1, vol. 25, p. 748. Hereinafter cited as *ORN*.

20 *Memoirs of William T Sherman, by Himself*, 2 vols. (New York, 1931), vol. 1, pp. 425-426.

taking part in a campaign in Arkansas that resulted in the capture of Helena. After leading a division in the XV Corps during the Vicksburg Campaign, Steele was made commander of the Department of Arkansas and ordered to clear the state of organized enemy forces. He captured Little Rock in September 1863, and the following spring was ordered by Grant to collaborate with Banks in the campaign up Red River.[21] After being informed of his role, Maj. Gen. Frederick Steele began making excuses as to why he could not participate. The election of state officers had been scheduled for March 14 and "the President is very anxious it should be a success," wrote Steele. "Without the assistance of the troops to distribute the poll-books, with the oath of allegiance, and to protect the voters at the polls, it cannot succeed."[22]

Then there was the problem of absent veterans. Part of his command had returned home on furlough and, as Steele noted, "matters in the Army are influenced so much by political intrigue, it is not certain that these troops will return to my command."[23]

In addition, he complained about impassable roads, ubiquitous Southern guerillas, and a depleted countryside that was so ravaged by war that it could not properly sustain his army. Wishing to circumvent his original commitment to drive southwest and meet up with Banks, Steele instead offered to engage in a long-range demonstration that promised to draw Confederate troops away from Banks' front.[24]

Although he was an experienced military officer and a graduate of West Point, Steele was not the most aggressive of Union generals, a trait that would have to be in steady supply for such a move to succeed. He also believed he had more than enough problems in Arkansas without having to take on an expedition into Louisiana.

While Steele was busy giving reasons why he could not participate in the planned expedition, Grant was promoted to general-in-chief of the Union armies, which proved to be a bad omen for the hesitant Steele. He was no longer dealing with the ambivalent, elbow-scratching Halleck. Grant solved the problem immediately by telegraphing Steele the following: "Move your force in full cooperation with General N. P. Banks' attack on Shreveport. A mere

---

21 Ezra Warner, *Generals in Blue* (Baton Rouge, 1964), p. 474.

22 *OR* 34, pt. 2, p. 448.

23 Ibid., p. 246.

24 Ibid., p. 576.

demonstration will not be sufficient."[25] With this terse telegraph message, the last component in the planned expedition was in place.

After Grant's thorny telegram pricked him into action, Steele, albeit reluctantly, began to assemble his force and slowly move overland toward Shreveport from Little Rock and Fort Smith via Arkadelphia. The stage was finally set for a combined movement of large field elements from three different military departments, supported by one of the largest concentrations of naval might ever assembled in North America.

On March 10, 1864, Admiral Porter's fleet assembled at the mouth of Red River near Simmesport. Porter's assemblage of vessels was an impressive array of ironclads, tinclads, and transports. The ironclads, his most powerful ships, numbered thirteen in all: *Essex, Benton, Lafayette, Choctaw, Chillicothe, Ozark, Louisville, Carondelet, Eastport, Pittsburg, Mound City, Osage,* and *Neosho.* Tinclads, light draft and lightly armored gunboats that would be useful in the shallow and often treacherous confines of the Red River, were also well-represented in Porter's fleet. This included the following ships: *Cricket, Gazelle, Signal, Juliet, Lexington, Black Hawk*—Admiral Porter's flagship—*Covington, Ouachita, Fort Hindman,* and *Avenge.* Among the other vessels was a steamer named *Black Hawk,* which was used by General Banks as his flagship during the expedition (not to be confused with the tinclad of the same name used by Porter).[26]

The admiral took his orders to support Banks seriously. He had stripped the inland navy based on the Mississippi River and its upper tributaries for this expedition and was "determined there should be no want of floating batteries for the troops to fall back on in case of disaster."[27] The ironclads, together with the tinclads, would act as the primary protection for the vessels carrying men, munitions, and supplies for the campaign. All of them were needed to help make the effort a success.

---

25 Ibid., pt. 2, p. 616.

26 Rear Admiral David D. Porter, "The Mississippi Flotilla in the Red River Expedition," in Robert U. Johnson and Clarence C. Buel, eds., *Battles and Leaders of the Civil War,* 4 vols. (New York, 1884-1889), vol. 4, p. 366. Porter, *Naval History,* pp. 494-533. Porter lists the vessels in the Mississippi Squadron on pp. 548-553. Other support ships accompanying Porter included: *Benefit* (naval transport), *Emerald* (transport), *Rob Roy* (transport), *Warner* (quartermaster's boat), *Champion No. 3* (pump boat), *Champion No. 5* (pump boat), and several transports carrying troops munitions and supplies.

27 Porter, *Naval History* p. 494.

Library of Congress

Admiral David D. Porter

The next day, March 11, army veteran Brig. Gen. Andrew J. Smith and his 10,000 men from Sherman's army joined Porter at the mouth of Red River. On 21 transports Smith brought with him fifteen regiments of infantry and two batteries of light artillery from the XVI Corps, six regiments of infantry and one battery of artillery from the XVII Corps, and Alfred W. Ellet's Marine Brigade. It was a formidable array of veterans, and Banks would need them all.[28]

Admiral Porter, although eager and optimistic about the expedition a few weeks earlier, grew suddenly pessimistic upon seeing the entrance to Red River. In later years and with the benefit of hindsight of his journey up the river, Porter described the waterway as "the most treacherous of all rivers; there is no counting on it, according to the rules which govern other streams, and when you bet your all that there would be a rise, ten to one the water would be lower than ever. Therefore it would require great judgment to properly enter upon an expedition in that quarter if vessels of any size were to accompany it."[29] While

28 *OR* 34, pt. 2, p. 554; ibid., pt. 1, p. 168.

29 Porter, *Incidents,* p. 213.

waiting on the arrival of Smith, Porter inspected the river and may well have wished he had not been so eager to assist in the campaign. The water level at the mouth was so low that the largest of his vessels—those with the deepest drafts—would have difficulty maneuvering over the sand bar at the entrance of the stream.[30]

The admiral's growing pessimism was well-founded. The Red River was one of the largest silt bearing streams in North America. Even today, within a period of hours, its shifting and unpredictable actions create immense quantities of sand and sand bars that dramatically lower water levels and make for treacherous navigation. Porter's melancholia only worsened when he learned that the Confederates, in anticipation of a Union naval invasion up Red River, had undertaken the completion of Fort De Russy, 30 miles south of Alexandria near the small hamlet of Marksville. Earlier in the war, Confederate General E. Kirby Smith, commander of the Trans-Mississippi Department, had ordered that Fort De Russy be built. Over the ensuing months the intended bastion had fallen into disrepair; Kirby again ordered the defensive emplacement rebuilt and expanded.[31] Work to complete the fort began immediately and by the time the Union forces arrived off Red River in mid-March, the earthen works of De Russy had been strengthened by casemates shielded with railroad iron.[32] The bastion, armed with eight heavy siege guns and two field pieces, was manned by 200 infantry under Col. William Byrd, in addition to the fort's gun crews.[33] Deep rifle pits were dug between the earthen works and the river to protect the gunners, and Colonel Byrd's infantry were stationed in these protective depressions. By all accounts it appeared to present a powerful obstacle.[34]

As a forward line of defense for Fort De Russy, the Confederate engineers had created a very strong obstruction to block navigation on the liver from downstream. This obstruction, located eight or nine miles south of the fort near what Porter called the "Bend of the Rappiones," was in a hairpin turn of the river.[35] The impediment was formidable, built of heavy wooden pilings driven into the stream bed completely across the river; a second line was added, shorter

---

30   Porter, *Incidents,* p. 213.

31   Ludwell H. Johnson, *Red River Campaign: Politics and Cotton in the Civil War* (Baltimore, 1958), pp. 87-88.

32   Thomas O. Selfridge, "The Navy in the Red River," *Battles and Leaders*, 4, p. 362.

33   Richard Taylor, *Destruction and Reconstruction* (New York, 1992), p. 180.

34   Ibid. p. 181.

35   Porter, *Naval History*, p. 496.

in height. The two lines were braced together and strengthened with ties. Attached to this structure was a raft of trees and timber from the bottom of the stream to its surface. According to Porter, the Confederates had cut down "a forest of trees" upstream and allowed them to pile up behind the structure.[36] The Confederates also drove pilings into the riverbed downstream from the main line of obstructions. The Southerners hoped that these obstacles would deny any vessel a clear channel of navigation on an already shallow and difficult waterway.[37]

When Smith arrived, Porter informed him of the difficulties his reconnaissance effort had uncovered. The news must have dampened Smith's optimism as well. He in turn added further frustrating news to the situation. He had received a wire from Banks that "the heavy rains had so delayed his column that he would not be able to reach Alexandria before March 21."[38] The expedition was not beginning on an auspicious note. The newly discovered barriers, however, did not long deter the two experienced veterans.

David Dixon Porter had a family tradition to uphold—five generations of Porters had served in the navy, most in positions of command and distinction. David Dixon, the second of four sons, was born on June 18, 1813, in Chester, Pennsylvania. He obtained his education at Columbia College, Washington, D.C., and thereafter accompanied his father, at the age of 10 years, on an expedition to the West Indies for the suppression of pirates. He later served as a midshipman in the Mexican Navy. Porter entered the United States Navy in 1829 as midshipman and cruised the Mediterranean conducting coastal surveys. He also gathered experience doing the same type of work along the coast of South America. Porter served throughout the Mexican War, first as lieutenant and then as commander of *Spitfire*.

When the Civil War broke out, Porter was placed in command of the steam frigate *Powhatan* and ordered to Pensacola, Florida, to assist the Gulf Squadron in blockading the difficult southern coast. In November 1861, Porter was appointed to the rank of Commander and placed in charge of a fleet of 21 schooners and five steamers. Six months later, in April 1862, Porter's fleet, in conjunction with the fleet of Flag Officer David G. Farragut, bombarded Forts Jackson and St. Philip below New Orleans on the Mississippi River, reducing those bastions and eventually capturing New Orleans. Five months later he was

---

36 Ibid.

37 Porter, *Incidents*, p. 214.

38 *OR* 34, pt. 1, p. 304.

appointed Rear Admiral and sent to command the Mississippi Squadron. The career navy officer assisted Sherman in the capture of Arkansas Post, bombarded the Confederate forts at Grand Gulf, and rendered invaluable service to Grant during the Vicksburg Campaign.

Porter's successes were too numerous and his personality too fiery to concede that the obstructions confronting his ships on Red River would arrest his ascension of that stream. He had a family tradition to honor and uphold, and he was supremely confident—perhaps too confident—that no obstacle was too formidable to prevent him from achieving his goal.

Brigadier General Andrew J. Smith was made of the same metal as Porter, though of less conspicuous genes. Born on a farm in Bucks County, Pennsylvania, in 1815, Smith was a dedicated Unionist. After graduation from West Point in 1838, he served in the 1st Dragoons in the Western territories. Smith was commissioned colonel of the 2nd California Cavalry when the war started and eventually became chief of cavalry under Halleck. After steady service in the Western Theater, which included solid service in the Vicksburg Campaign, Smith was neither fearful in his actions or tentative in his style. He and Porter were excellent officers, and both would prove their military worth during the expedition.

Forgetting Nathaniel Banks for a time, the two veterans held a conference and developed a plan of action to overcome the Confederate river obstacles and Fort De Russy. They agreed to act in conjunction against the latter, with "the army in the rear by land and the navy by river."[39] It was further agreed that whoever got to Fort De Russy first would wait on the support of the other to arrive before an attack was made. Smith was confident he would have little difficulty moving against the Rebel fortification, and Porter was also convinced the river obstructions facing him could be rapidly surmounted.

Entering Red River from the Mississippi was not as simple as Porter hoped it would be. By a quirk of nature, Red River does not flow directly into the Mississippi, but instead empties first into the Atchafalaya Bayou. On March 12, Smith floated his transports into the Atchafalya and reached Simmesport, where he disembarked his men. He immediately began his overland march to Fort De Russy, meeting only minor resistance from Confederate Maj. Gen. John G. Walker's Division.[40] After conducting a reconnaissance just north of

---

39 Ibid.

40 Ibid., pp. 304, 598-601. According to John Walker's report of Smith's landing, Brig. Gen. William R. Scurry's Brigade was dispatched to drive the Unionists back aboard their

Simmesport in the Fort Humbug area, during which he discovered the enemy force in front of him (Brig. Gen. William R. Scurry's Brigade) was small and in retreat, a confident Smith sent his empty transports back to join Porter's squadron. The campaign had begun in earnest.[41]

While Smith was entering the Atchafalaya and disembarking his troops at Simmesport, Porter was beginning his ascent of Red River. Almost immediately he encountered the obstructions the Confederates had built in the river below Fort De Russy. No better description of what transpired exists than Porter's own words. "When I first saw these lower obstructions I began to think that the enemy had blocked the game on us," remembered the aging admiral, "and how astonished General Smith would be when he arrived in front of the forts and found no gun-boats to help him!" Porter continued his narrative with the following recollection:

> It would be mortifying to me, and might be disastrous to him; but, after looking at the obstructions carefully for a few minutes, I said, Bosh! to think of these fellows trying to block out a party who had been on the Deer Creek expedition in the Yazoo country, who had pulled up Titanic trees by the roots and removed giant oaks from their paths when cut down to stop their progress; who forced their way up through seventy-five miles of logs, canebrakes, and small willows under a hot fire from sharp-shooters! Why, this is simply silly, and shows how these Confederates waste their time to no purpose. What indefatigable energy! What a waste of money and horse-power! Blessed is the power of steam, by which we can undo, in a few hours, the labor of years; and blessed is the edict of the gods, that 'whom they wish to destroy make idiots of themselves,' or words to that effect!

Porter's recollection, of course, is colored with the all the benefits that hindsight brings when one looks backward in time and knows how events eventually played out. He concluded his appraisal by overly simplifying what was surely a difficult and dangerous undertaking:

---

vessels, but the discovery of the strength of Smith's contingent instead prompted a Rebel retrograde to Moreauville, eleven miles west of Simmesport.

41 Ibid., pp. 304, 599.

What folly for any one to attempt to keep a naval force out of harbors and rivers by torpedoes and barricades when they have not heavy forts to protect the obstructions, or a superior naval force! You might as well try to obstruct Niagara Falls with tooth-picks or quill pop-guns. When I made up my mind about these obstructions which looked so formidable, I simply gave the order, "Clear that away!"[42]

As brief as Porter's delay was, it prevented his fleet from reaching the fort ahead of Smith's advancing troops. After bivouacking for the night about four miles from Simmesport, Smith had his men up and marching by 3:00 a.m. for Fort De Russy. By that afternoon Smith had formed a line of battle with the First and Second Brigades, Third Division, XVI Corps. A reconnaissance revealed the fort to be but thinly manned. The veteran temporized for a short while before deciding to ignore his agreement to wait for Porter's support. Instead, he ordered his veterans to assault the under-manned fortification. Brigadier General Joseph A. Mower, a Vermonter and veteran of Iuka, Corinth, and Vicksburg, commanded the Third Division. Mower's men spearheaded the attack that overwhelmed the approximately 300 Confederates defending De Russy. Within about ten minutes of the order to charge the fighting sputtered to an end. Confederate losses amounted to five killed, four wounded and 250 captured, together with the loss of ten artillery pieces. Smith's Federals lost only three killed and 35 wounded. The complete victory belonged to the infantry alone; Porter's fleet arrived after the surrender of the fort.[43] The defensive hopes placed by Southerners in De Russy were misplaced, as Maj. Gen. Richard Taylor later noted when he wrote, "Thus much for our Red River Gibraltar."[44]

On March 15, Joseph Mower's XVI Corps division re-embarked on its transports and, together with Porter's fleet, headed northwest to take possession of Alexandria. Andrew Smith remained behind with Brig. Gen. Kilby Smith's command to supervise the destruction of De Russy. Porter, attempting to capitalize on the quick fall of De Russy, ordered his fastest gunboat, *Eastport*, under the command of Lt. Cdr. S. L. Phelps, ahead of the balance of the fleet to try and seize any Confederate vessels that had moved upstream after the fall of

---

42 Porter, *Incidents*, pp. 214-215.

43 *OR* 34, pt. 1, pp. 305, 313, 338-339. Walker's Texas Division was outflanked by A. J. Smith when Smith crossed Bayou De Glaize and marched upon De Russy. Smith left Brig. Gen. T. Kilby Smith's division to watch Walker while the balance of the Union column moved upon Fort De Russy. Welcher, *The Union Army*, 2, p. 750; Walter G. Smith, ed., *Life and Letters of Thomas Kilby Smith* (New York, 1898), p. 358.

44 Taylor, *Destruction and Reconstruction*, p. 181.

De Russy. The message ordering Phelps on this mission, however, was delayed and prevented Phelps from reaping any inland river prizes.[45] Shortly after their arrival in Alexandria on the afternoon of March 15, the Confederate vessels moved further upstream and out of reach of *Eastport*. Only one Confederate ship, a steamer, was lost during the withdrawal. Because of the negligence of the pilot, she grounded on what General Taylor called "falls," and was burned to keep her out of Union hands. In addition to the steamer, the Confederates lost three field pieces, which were accidentally left behind north of Alexandria.[46] Porter's fleet reached Alexandria four days before its scheduled rendezvous with Banks' column. By the morning of the 16th, nine gunboats had arrived and Porter ordered Lt. Cdr. Thomas O. Selfridge, captain of *Osage*, to land with 180 men and to take possession of the city. The town changed hands peacefully.[47]

Realizing that a direct confrontation with the advancing Unionists would be futile, Major General Taylor personally supervised Alexandria's evacuation. Public property was loaded on steamers and sent above the shallows and rapids that partially obstructed the river upstream of Alexandria. It was during this evacuation that the Confederates lost the steamer mentioned above.[48] There was nothing left for the Federals to do but disembark and walk through the town's deserted streets.

Richard Taylor was retreating northwest to Natchitoches, but it was not a retreat brought about by the defeat of his army. It was not in Taylor's character to give up so easily. The wily and patient general ordered the withdrawal to provide him with the time he needed to gather his scattered forces for a pitched confrontation against the Federals at a time and place of his choosing. In Taylor Banks would find an adversary almost as deadly as Stonewall Jackson.

Bank's opponent was the son of President Zachary Taylor and the brother of Jefferson Davis' first wife, Sarah Knox Taylor. He was born on an estate near Louisville, Kentucky, in 1826. He attended both Harvard and Yale, and spent much of his youth with his father at frontier posts and serving as his military secretary during the Mexican War. In the 1850s, he established himself as a sugar planter in Louisiana and began dabbling in local politics, an interest that carried him into the state senate in 1856 and 1861. At the outbreak of the Civil

---

45 Selfridge, "The Navy in the Red River," *Battles and Leaders*, p. 362.

46 Taylor, *Destruction and Reconstruction*, pp. 181-183; *OR* 34, pt. 1, p. 506.

47 Selfridge, "The Navy in the Red River," *Battles and Leaders*, p. 362.

48 *OR* 34, pt. 1, pp. 506, 561.

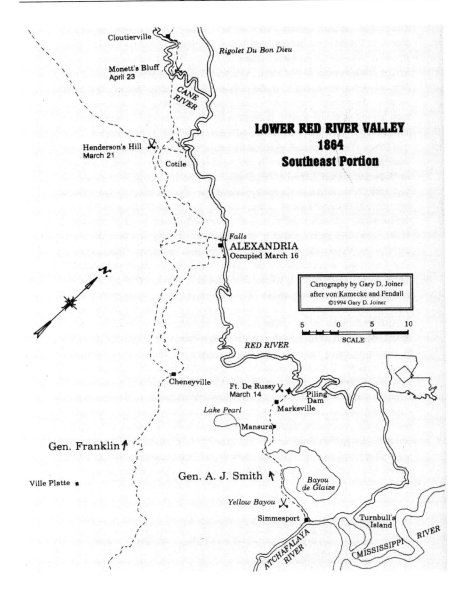

Cloutierville

Rigolet Du Bon Dieu

Monett's Bluff
April 23

CANE
RIVER

LOWER RED RIVER VALLEY
1864
Southeast Portion

Henderson's Hill
March 21

Cotile

Falls
■ **ALEXANDRIA**
Occupied March 16

Cartography by Gary D. Joiner
after von Kamecke and Fendall
©1994 Gary D. Joiner

RED RIVER

5   0   5   10
SCALE

Cheneyville

Ft. De Russy
March 14
Piling
Dam
Lake Pearl   Marksville

Mansura

Gen. Franklin↑

Ville Platte ■

Gen. A. J. Smith ↖   *Bayou
de Glaize*

Yellow Bayou

Simmesport   Turnbull's
Island   RIVER

ATCHAFALAYA
RIVER   MISSISSIPPI

War, Taylor was appointed colonel of the 9th Louisiana Infantry. Although he arrived too late to participate in the First Battle of Manassas, he was nonetheless promoted to brigadier general exactly three months later. His best service in Virginia was rendered at the head of the Louisiana Brigade under Maj. Gen. Thomas J. "Stonewall" Jackson in the Shenandoah Valley fighting during the spring of 1862. Taylor led his brigade in two well-timed assaults against the enemy, winning the praise of both his men and fellow officers. His steady stream of successes, which included service in several of the Seven Days' Battles outside Richmond that summer, resulted in a promotion to major general on July 28, 1862. He was sent west from Virginia to his home state as commander of the District of West Louisiana that August. An experienced combat commander with a firm determination to succeed, Taylor's exploits both in Virginia and west of the Mississippi River upheld his family's proud military reputation. He was also headstrong, arrogant, quick-tempered, and extremely intelligent.[49]

And he immediately clashed with his superior, Gen. Edmund Kirby Smith, commander of the Trans-Mississippi Department. Taylor disagreed strongly with Smith's political policies and would later write, "The commander of the Trans-Mississippi Department displayed much ardor in the establishment of bureaus, and on a scale proportional rather to the extent of his territory than to the smallness of his force. His staff surpassed in numbers that of Von Moltke during the war with France; and, to supply the demands of bureaus and staff, constant details from the infantry were called for, to the great discontent of officers in the field. Hydrocephalus at Shreveport produced atrophy elsewhere."[50]

Although the conflict between the two officers continued to alternately smolder and flame, Taylor, as the tactical commander in the field, was determined that Smith's policies would not hamper his efforts to bring Nathaniel Banks' Federals to disaster in the swamps and woods of Louisiana. Faced with a superior enemy force, Taylor retreated, consolidated his forces, bided his time—and often ignored his superior.[51]

49   T. Michael Parish, "Richard Taylor," in William C. Davis, ed., *The Confederate General*, 6 vols. (Harrisburg, 1991), vol. 6, pp. 29-30.

50   Taylor, *Destruction and Reconstruction*, p. 153.

51   After John Walker's Texas division fell back to Natchitoches, Taylor began assembling his forces at the Carrol Jones residence, a farmstead owned by a prominent free black on the road between Opelousas and Fort Jessup, about 30 miles northwest of Alexandria. His force at this time consisted of two small divisions numbering only about 7,000 men. In addition to Walker's brigades, Taylor formed another mini-division with the brigades of Brig. Gen. Alfred Mouton and Brig. Gen. Camille J. Polignac, the latter of which was summoned by Taylor from the Tensas River line after Walker retreated to Natchitoches. T. Michael

David Porter had little difficulty ignoring the Union field commander, for Banks was not on the scene for the initial opening of Red River Campaign and would not arrive in the vicinity for another week. Frustrated by his recent experience on the river, Porter became increasingly upset with Banks' absence.[52] Instead of lying idle, Porter put his men and ships to good work seizing cotton as a prize of war. Federal legislation with respect to wartime trade had left the naval prize law intact and Porter was not going to miss what many viewed as a golden opportunity to acquire mountains of the valuable staple.[53] Naval officer Thomas Selfridge later wrote in his memoirs that the "incentive of prize money naturally influenced the navy to be especially active."[54]

And active it was. Gunboats and barges were sent between Alexandria and the mouth of the Red River to gather all available cotton. The navy seized 300 bales from warehouses in Alexandria and sailors were sent ten miles inland in all directions, scouring the land for the prized white crop.[55] Cotton found unbaled was taken to local gins, where Federal sailors ran the machinery themselves. Lacking a means of transporting the cotton on land, the Union tars "liberated" Southern mules and used them for hauling the cotton—after painting large "USN" letters on the sides of the beasts. A certain bit of waggery was involved while collecting the cotton, for after it was baled, the sailors branded each parcel with the letters "CSA," and below that, "USN." When Porter was asked what the lettering stood for, he replied, "Cotton Stealing Association of the United States Navy."[56]

The seized cotton was loaded onto barges and shipped to the admiralty court at Cairo, Illinois. In all, the navy seized some 3,000 bales by the time Banks arrived on Red River.[57]

Parrish, *Richard Taylor: Soldier Prince of Dixie* (Chapel Hill, 1992), p. 327; Welcher, *Union Army*, p. 750.

52 Porter, *Naval History*, p. 499.

53 Joint Committee on the Conduct of the War, pp. 18, 71, 74, 224-225.

54 Selfridge, Thomas O., *What Finer Tradition: the Memoirs of Thomas O. Selfridge, Jr. Rear Admiral, U.S.N.* (Columbia, 1987), p. 96.

55 *Official Report Relative to the Conduct of Federal Troops in Western Louisiana, During the Invasions of 1863 and 1864* (Shreveport, 1865), p. 84; *OR* 34, pt. 2, p. 655.

56 Joint Committee on the Conduct of the war, pp. 11, 18, and 74, *OR* 34, pt. 3, pp. 18-19. Wool and molasses were also seized as prizes of war.

57 John D. Winters, *The Civil War in Louisiana* (Baton Rouge, 1963), p. 331.

The first portion of Banks' army, one hundred men from Brig. Gen. Albert L. Lee's 5,000-man cavalry division, rode into the streets of Alexandria, Louisiana on March 19, the same day Banks' headquarters steamer, carrying his chief-of-staff Brig. Gen. Charles P. Stone and several other staff members, arrived in the captured city. The next day the main body of Lee's cavalry joined Banks' advance contingent in Alexandria. Banks, who had been delayed on departmental business matters in New Orleans, did not arrive until March 24, when he stepped onto the wharf at Alexandria from his steamer *Black Hawk*. His infantry, delayed by rain and muddy roads, slogged along from Franklin, Louisiana, to Alexandria, arriving in driblets over March 25-26. These soldiers consisted of the XIII Corps, commanded by Brig. Gen. Thomas E. G. Ransom, and the XIX Corps, under the command of Brig. Gen. William Emory. Major General William Buel Franklin, a veteran of the Virginia Theater and the official leader of the XIX Corps, had been in overall command of the army while Banks was absent in New Orleans.[58]

In spite of delays, both bureaucratic and natural in origin, the Union naval and army forces had come together to embark on an expedition that would hopefully take them to Shreveport and into the state of Texas. As the principal historian of the campaign, Ludwell H. Johnson, wrote: "It was an impressive display of military might—the greatest in the history of the Southwest."[59] In addition to Porter's 13 ironclads, four tinclads, and five other armed vessels, the combined forces included the army's transports and quartermaster boats, a total of 60 vessels mounting 210 guns.[60] The land forces included a detachment from William T. Sherman's Army of the Tennessee, consisting of two divisions of the XVI Corps and one division of the XVII Corps.[61] From the Department of the Gulf came two divisions of the XIII Corps and two from the XIX Corps, plus Lee's cavalry division. These detachments amounted to 14,250 infantry and

---

58 James Ewer, *The Third Massachusetts Cavalry in the War for the Union* (Maplewood, 1903), p. 136; Winters, *Civil War in Louisiana*, p. 330; *OR* 34, pt. 1, pp. 426-427.

59 Johnson, *Red River Campaign*, p. 99.

60 See the organizational table provided in Johnson and Buel, *Battles and Leaders*, 4. p. 366.

61 These units were involved with the capture of Fort De Russy. The XVI Corps divisions were commanded Brig. Gen. Joseph Mower, and the XVII Corps division by T. Kilby Smith. The detachment from Sherman's army also originally included Brig. Gen. Alfred W. Ellet's Marine Brigade, but Ellet was ordered back to Vicksburg on March 27, leaving about 8,000 effectives with Banks from the Army of the Tennessee. *OR* 34, pt. 1, p. 168; Richard B. Irwin, "The Red River Campaign," *Battles and Leaders*, 4, pp. 350-351.

artillery and 3,900 cavalry. Although they were to see no action, 2,500 black troops of the Corps d'Afrique were also present. Engineer and escort troops brought the final total of land forces to 32,500 effectives, with 90 guns.[62]

Although Banks had an impressive military force under his command, he faced a number of vexing problems upon his arrival in Alexandria. Porter's cotton-collecting activates infuriated him and had a demoralizing effect on his troops since, according to the law, the army was not permitted (as was the navy) to confiscate the fiber for prize money. In a postwar appearance before the Committee on the Conduct of War, Maj. David C. Houston testified: "It was rather demoralizing to the soldiers to see the navy seizing the cotton for prize on land, while they did not get any."[63] Banks had no authority to stop Porter from seizing the cotton, and thus the race began. Who could get the most cotton, the navy or the army? The navy wanted it for prize money, the army (actually Banks) wanted it for the Treasury Department. Banks was even more

upset with Porter because his (Banks') headquarters steamer had brought with it not only his staff but a bevy of cotton speculators. The sight must have been amusing and absurd: sailors and soldiers racing all over the area trying to see who could get to the cotton first. In some respects it is surprising that war did not break out in Alexandria between the United States Navy and the United States Army.

In addition to the brewing cotton fiasco, two days after he arrived in Alexandria Banks received a letter from Grant, the new general-in-chief, admonishing the political general to act quickly and decisively in his bid to seize Shreveport. "I regard the success of your present move as of great importance in reducing the number of troops necessary for protecting the navigation of the Mississippi River," wrote Grant. "It is also important that Shreveport should be taken as soon as possible. This done, send Brig. Gen. A. J. Smith with his command back to Memphis as soon as possible." He told Banks that if he did not think he could take Shreveport by the end of April, he must return A. J. Smith's command to Sherman by the middle of the month "even if it leads to the abandonment of the main object of your expedition." Finally, Grant stated that if Shreveport was captured, Banks was to hold the city and the Red River with only those troops necessary to do so, and send the remainder of his command to New Orleans to be ready to participate in the move against Mobile. It seems clear that

62   Abstract of U.S. troops composing the Red River Expedition, March 31 and April 30, 1864, *OR* 34, pt. 1, p. 168.

63   Joint Committee on the Conduct of the War, pp. 18, 74.

Grant did not believe any significant results would be obtained by Banks along Red River.[64] As with Steele in Arkansas, Grant was pushing Banks to the wall. If Banks did not move quickly, he would lose a substantial portion of his army. The April deadline loomed near, and Banks was not immune to the pressure that such a restriction placed upon him. Suddenly, his military reputation in general, and his political status in particular, was on the line. Failure in the field along Red River could well mean personal military disaster in the army and the end of his chance to gain the presidency.

The final problem Banks faced, and perhaps his most significant dilemma, was the river itself: its expected annual rise had failed to materialize. For the first time in nine years, Red River had not risen to flood stage as was anticipated.[65] Instead of rising water levels, Porter reported that the stream was falling at an average of one inch per hour.[66] To make matters worse, this part of the river contained a number of irregularities in the channel bottom that resulted in a series of rapids. When the river was at a low stage, these rapids created obstructions to navigation potentially greater than the obstacle at Fort De Russy. Unlike De Russy's man-made barrier, nature's impediment could not simply be yanked apart by Admiral Porter's men. Realizing the significance of the river's failure to rise, Banks grew concerned that Porter would not or could not fulfill his obligation to support his infantry.

And Porter's feet had indeed grown cold. He expressed to Banks his reluctance to send his vessels into the upper Red River because of the hazards the low water posed to his ships. Simply put, it might be difficult or impossible to get them back down again. Banks reminded Porter that the presence of his navy was necessary for the success of the expedition, and that the War Department was counting on Porter to assist Banks in every possible way. He also appealed to Porter's weakness for cotton: the capture of Shreveport would be added prize money for the navy. The appeal offered by the Massachusetts politician proved effective, and Porter agreed to steam his ships up the Red—even if it meant "I should lose all my boats."[67]

With this commitment made, Porter began the task of getting his fleet over the shallow rapids just north of Alexandria. Against the advice of his

64 *OR* 34, pt. 2, pp. 494, 610-611.

65 Robert L. Kerby, *Kirby Smith's Confederacy: The Trans-Mississippi South, 1863-1865* (Tuscaloosa, 1972), p. 297.

66 Porter, *Naval History*, p. 500.

67 Joint Committee on the Conduct of the War, pp. 8-9, *ORN* 26, p. 50.

experienced pilot, Wellington W. Withenbury, the admiral ordered *Eastport*, his heaviest ironclad, to negotiate the waters first. "I remarked to Admiral Porter then," Withenbury later testified, "that it was bad policy to put the largest boat into the chute first, as she might get aground, and if she did it would hinder the passage of the other vessels." Despite his pilot's sound advice, Porter would have none of it. "I want you to go on board and take her over the falls," he ordered.[68]

As Withenbury predicted, Porter's decision proved to be a bad one. *Eastport* mounted a full head of steam and started over the rapids, where she struck the rocks and immediately grounded. For almost three days soldiers and sailors used hawsers in an attempt to work the vessel free from the river's tight grip. After she was finally liberated on March 26, *Eastport* and eleven other gunboats steamed through the rapids and headed into the upper reaches of the Red River.[69] As difficult as it was getting the warships over the rapids, it was not until April 3 that the last of the 30 transports succeeded in navigating the speedy shallows. Fortunately for Porter and surprisingly to everyone, only one vessel was lost. The ship was the hospital boat *Woodford*, which wrecked on the shoals and had to be burned.[70]

On the same day Porter began his move up Red River above Alexandria, the Federal army began its march northwest toward Grand Ecore and Natchitoches. Albert Lee's cavalry, which was scouting for the army, led the way as Andrew J. Smith's Army of the Tennessee contingent left Alexandria on March 26 and tramped its way to Cotile Landing, some 21 miles north of Alexandria. There, Andrew's men gladly embarked on Porter's transports for the trip upriver. The XIII Corps and Emory's division of the XIX Corps, all under the command of William B. Franklin, marched after Smith's men the next day.[71] By April 3, these troops were encamped in or near Grand Ecore, 50 miles northwest of Alexandria.

Grand Ecore, a small and insignificant village consisting of only a few dwellings and no commercial establishments, was constructed on the west bank of Red River approximately four miles north of Natchitoches. Banks did not

---

68   Joint Committee on the Conduct of the War, p. 275.

69   *ORN* 26, p. 50. In addition to *Eastport*, the ships accompanying Banks upriver included the tinclads *Cricket* and *Fort Hindman*; the wooden warship *Lexington*; and the ironclads *Mound City, Chillicothe, Carondelet, Pittsburg, Ozark, Neosho, Louisville*, and *Osage*.

70   Ibid.

71   Welcher, *The Union Army*, p. 752; *OR* 34, pt. 1, pp. 181, 214, 307.

arrive at the hamlet until the evening of April 3, when he steamed up on his headquarters boat *Black Hawk*. His brief delay in reaching his army's vanguard had been caused by local elections he oversaw in Alexandria, and because *Black Hawk* had to stop and assist the ponderous *Eastport*, which had run aground a second time.[72] It was at this small, peaceful riverside village that Banks made the decision that would lead to both the worst Federal defeat on Louisiana soil during the Civil War and the demise of his hopes of winning the Republican nomination for the White House.

This far into the campaign, the route the army had taken northwest into Louisiana had closely followed Red River. This allowed the army to remain in close contact with the navy during its march from Alexandria, in constant communication with its transports and supply boats. Banks also had the comfort of knowing that Porter's water-borne guns were near at hand to support his infantry. At Grand Ecore, however, the road to Shreveport turned west, *away* from the river, moving inland toward White's Store and Fort Jessup. Unless there was another route by land, the army would have little choice but to leave the comfort and security offered by the presence of Porter's fleet on Red River and strike out on its own. Banks was faced with perhaps his most important strategic and logistical decision of the campaign. His inquiries about the road to Shreveport confirmed it was indeed the most direct land-based route available. He also explored whether it would be possible to "cross the river at that point [Grand Ecore] and go up on the other side." Although the plan was feasible, he was informed that such a move would consume an additional three days. Banks knew that if he followed the shortest inland route, his army would be out of touch with the river and Porter's ships until he reached Shreveport.[73] Banks was encouraged by some members of his staff to undertake a reconnaissance in the hopes of discovering a road to Shreveport that would keep his army in close contact with the river and the navy, but he rejected the idea because it would waste time that he considered too precious to squander. And so Banks made what was probably the most important mistake of his military career. With this decision, the Red River Expedition took a completely different turn, and ultimately resulted in the defeat of the Federal army.[74]

---

72 Joint Committee on the Conduct of the War, pp. 282,286.

73 Ibid. pp. 286-287.

74 Ibid., p. 35. Had Banks undertaken this reconnaissance, he would have discovered a useable river road leading through the bayou and swamps to Shreveport.

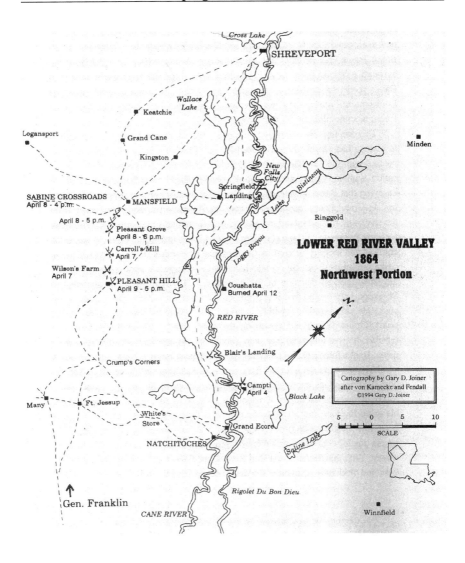

Cross Lake

SHREVEPORT

Wallace Lake

■ Keatchie

Logansport
■

■ Grand Cane

Kingston ■

New Falls City

Springfield
Landing

Minden
■

SABINE CROSSROADS
April 8 - 4 p.m.   ■ MANSFIELD

Ringgold
■

April 8 - 5 p.m.

Pleasant Grove
April 8 - 6 p.m.

Carroll's Mill
April 7

Wilson's Farm
April 7

PLEASANT HILL
April 9 - 5 p.m.

Coushatta
Burned April 12

**LOWER RED RIVER VALLEY
1864
Northwest Portion**

RED RIVER

Blair's Landing

Crump's Corners

Cartography by Gary D. Joiner
after von Kamecke and Fendall
©1994 Gary D. Joiner

Many
■

■ Ft. Jessup

Campti
April 4

Black Lake

5   0   5   10

White's
Store

Grand Ecore

SCALE

NATCHITOCHES

Rigolet Du Bon Dieu

↑
Gen. Franklin

CANE RIVER

Winnfield
■

The orders were given and on April 6, the army began its march out of Grand Ecore, heading inland (west) away from the river. Lee's cavalry once again took the lead and was followed by Franklin's infantry. The column was heavily encumbered by wagons, 300 with the cavalry, and another 700 accompanying the infantry. Andrew J. Smith's troops formed the rear of the column and did not leave Grand Ecore until the next day. The Corps d'Afrique, under the command of Col. William H. Dickey, was assigned to guard wagons, and Col. Oliver P. Gooding's brigade of cavalry was stationed to guard the rear and left column of the marching army.[75] Banks planned to meet the fleet in three days about 30 miles south of Shreveport and west of Red River at Springfield Landing. This landing was six miles northeast of the town of Mansfield, where a network of roads joined together to form a vital logistical junction. Mansfield was also the largest town between Natchitoches and Shreveport. While Banks was marching on Springfield Landing, Porter would travel upriver to Loggy Bayou almost due east of Springfield Landing and make contact with the army as it moved north from Mansfield. Although it was a potentially dangerous plan, its success would all but ensure the capture of Shreveport and pave the way for a major Union victory in Louisiana.[76]

After waiting for four days for the river to rise, Porter finally began his move up Red River on April 7. Still concerned about the river's shallowness and the distinct possibility that his heaviest ships would ground and obstruct the river or be captured by the enemy, Porter left six of his largest gunboats at Grand Ecore. Accompanying his warships was a fleet of 20 transports loaded with supplies and munitions, together with the division of Brig. Gen. T. Kilby Smith. Smith's 2,500 men were taken up the river to guard the unarmed vessels. Upon reaching Springfield Landing, Smith was to make a reconnaissance-in-force on the road leading from the landing to Mansfield with the intention of linking up with Banks' column.[77] The arduous twisting trip was 110 miles by river. Porter steamed upstream on his flagship *Cricket* accompanied by the ironclads *Osage*, *Neosho*, *Fort Hindman*, *Lexington*, and *Chillicothe*.[78]

75 *OR* 34, pt. 1, pp. 282, 322, 324, 331, 428, 445; Richard Irwin, *History of the Nineteenth Army Corps* (New York, 1892), p. 296.

76 Joint Committee on the Conduct of the War, pp. 210, 276, 323.

77 Ibid.

78 Selfridge, " The Navy in the Red River," *Battles and Leaders*, p. 363.

At 5:00 p.m. on April 7, the flotilla steamed into Campti, a short distance north of Grand Ecore, where Smith disembarked a regiment and reconnoitered the area. After making sure that the wooded banks were not hiding Taylor's Confederates, the regiment boarded the transports. Due to the grounding of the transport *Iberville*, however, the fleet did not get started again until 10:30 the next morning. The low water and narrow channels made for sluggish progress up the river, whose bottom was choked with stumps and precarious snags that posed serious danger to the ships. By 6:00 p.m. that evening, Porter managed to reach Coushatta Chute. Rightfully concerned about the possibility of a Rebel attack on the squadron, Smith disembarked a brigade under the command of Col. Lyman Ward to investigate a rumor that Confederate troops were in the area. Although Ward did encounter a small group of Confederates, the Southerners retreated in the face of the brigade.[79]

The fleet continued its move north at 9:00 a.m. on April 8. That day and the next Porter received rumors of a running inland battle many miles to the west, but there was no confirmation and it was assumed that the enemy was defeated and in retreat.[80] The naval flotilla reached Nine Mile Bend on the afternoon of April 9, and by afternoon of the next day the fleet pulled into the mouth of Loggy Bayou.[81]

There, Porter discovered that the Confederates had placed an old steamer, *New Falls City*, across the breadth of the river with her bow and stem resting 15 feet on the opposite banks and the midships hull lying on the bottom. A sandbar was beginning to form around the destroyed steamer. It was a clever way to damn up the narrow waterway at little or not cost. The admiral agreed, writing to Sherman, "[it] . . . made me laugh. It was the smartest thing I ever knew the rebels to do." He noted further, "An invitation in large letters to attend a ball in Shreveport was kindly left stuck up by the rebels, which invitation we were never able to accept."[82]

After designating which officers would work on removing the wrecked ship, Porter rode with Kilby Smith and his troops into the countryside to reconnoiter the area. At one point they observed several Confederates who, in turn, were observing them. Porter looked at Smith and said: "Banks has been defeated, or we wouldn't see those men. If Banks was still advancing, the

79   *OR* 34, pt. 1, p. 380.
80   *ORN* 26, p. 60.
81   *OR* 34, pt. 1, p. 380.
82   *ORN* 26, p. 60.

outposts would keep on the main road to Shreveport. If defeated, the enemy's lookouts would be watching for our arrival, and be ready to turn their whole force upon us, and it behooves us to be wary."[83] Porter and Smith agreed to create a feint by bringing artillery ashore together with some infantry and make a move toward the Confederates. Such a feint, it was hoped, would drive the pickets back. The maneuver was successful and the troops and artillery returned to the safety of the fleet. Shortly after this land action and before Porter could remove *New Falls City*, Capt. William H. C. Andres, escorted by 50 men from the 14th New York Cavalry, rode in from the west bearing dispatches from Banks. Porter's natural soldier's instinct had been right: Banks "had been badly whipped and was in full retreat to Grand Ecore." According to Porter, the courier also carried orders for Smith's troops and the fleet to return to Grand Ecore at once.[84]

Although the order to retreat was given by Andres verbally, if Banks had met with a serious setback, the fleet was in peril. They quickly decided to head south before the enemy could effectively blockade the river and prevent their retreat. The last thing Porter could afford was to be trapped upriver and risk losing both the fleet and Smith's infantry division.[85]

The banks of Red River in this stretch of the stream were substantially higher than the ship's pilot houses, thus favoring Rebel sharpshooters and artillerists who, according to Porter, "could annoy us with impunity." The admiral ordered artillery placed on the upper decks of the transports and barricades made of any materials available for firing positions for infantry. Porter, never a fool and not one to suffer fools gladly, took every precaution he could to protect his men and boats. With these preparations, the Union fleet began its arduous downstream passage from Loggy Bayou, the point of deepest Union naval penetration during the Red River Campaign.

The same obstacles that vexed Porter on his journey up the river—the narrow channel and shallow water—also frustrated his return down the waterway: These natural impediments forced the largest vessels to back down the river stern first for several miles before they could turn around. The mechanics of this type of movement over an extended course caused severe

83   Porter, *Naval History*, p. 502. Porter did not mention this incident in his official report of the campaign. Banks had indeed suffered a sharp tactical defeat at Mansfield (Sabine Crossroads) on April 8, and a strategic defeat the following day at Pleasant Hill.

84   *ORN* 26, p. 51.

85   *OR* 34, pt. 1, pp. 380, 452; pt. 3, pp. 98-99; *ORN* 26, pp. 51, 60; Abstract log of the *USS Rattler*, June 3-December 31, 1864, ibid., p. 798.

problems with steerage assemblies and major difficulties developed. Hazards in the stream bed and the sandbars native to Red River compounded this state of affairs.[86]

Almost immediately *Chillicothe* impaled herself on a large submerged stump, an accident that brought the entire fleet to a halt for more than two hours. After some difficulty *Black Hawk*, using *Chillicothe's* hawser, was able to extricate her.[87] Other boats suffered such additional ignominies as broken rudders and splintered paddles. On the late afternoon of April 11, musketry fire of Confederate sharpshooters under the command of Brig. Gen. St. John Richardson Liddell peppered the sides of *Benefit*, *Black Hawk*, and *Osage*. The gunboats replied, firing their large 11-inch guns into the thick pine trees lining the nearby riverbanks. Although neither side was able inflict substantial damage to the other, the constant threat of sudden attack from just a handful of yards away played havoc with the nerves of the Federal sailors.[88] That evening around 7:15, *Emerald* ran aground. The fleet finally reached Coushatta Chute around 8:00 p.m. and settled in for the night. It had been an exasperating day for Porter and his pilots.[89]

The situation did not change on the 12th. Almost immediately after getting underway *Lexington* collided with the transport *Rob Roy*, spearing her wheelhouse and launch and damaging her smoke stacks.[90] The sight of ships running into one another on a narrow river in wartime, to a disinterested observer, would have been amusing, a naval variation on the latter-day antics of the Keystone cops.

The fleet approached Blair's Landing, due west of Pleasant Hill and 45 miles north of Grand Ecore, later that day. As soon as they reached the landing a number of transports and gunboats ran aground, causing still another delay in Porter's attempt to carry his fleet out of harm's way. This particular grounding carried with it a very real danger, however, for the beached vessels were soon confronted by several Confederate regiments under the command of Brig. Gen. Thomas Green, who had been dispatched from the Pleasant Hill battlefield by

---

86   Edmund Newsome, *Experience in the War of the Great Rebellion* (Carbondale, 1880), p. 126.

87   Kerby, *Kirby Smith's Confederacy*, p. 309; Abstract log of *USS Chillicothe*, March 7-June 8, 1864, *ORN* 26, pp. 777-778.

88   *ORN* 26, pp. 778, 781, 789. For additional information regarding Confederate participation in this affair, see Liddell's report, *OR* 34, pt. 1, p. 633.

89   *OR* 34, pt, 1, p. 381.

90   Abstract log of *USS Lexington*, March 1-June 28, 1864, *ORN* 26, p. 789.

General Taylor to intercept the fleet.[91] Kilby Smith acted quickly by gathering guns from three of his transports and positioning them on the east side of the river. He immediately opened fire on Green and his men, who were seen approaching from some distance away. Green's troops took cover among the cottonwoods and pines and began to fire at the boats. Smith posted his men on the hurricane decks and had them well protected by cotton and hay bales and sacks of oats.

For two hours Blair's Landing was the hottest spot on Red River. The musket fire and artillery shells flew through the air, smokestacks collapsed, wheelhouse walls were destroyed, rudders splintered, bulkheads rattled, and decks spattered with blood. The transport *Hastings*, which was having her wheel repaired, and *Alice Vivian*, which was carrying 400 cavalry horses, suffered the bad luck of being aground in midstream when Green's men struck; they were the first to suffer Confederate fire. Not far behind were *Emerald* and *Clara Bell*, which had stopped to give assistance to *Alice Vivian* and got caught in the barrage of musket balls and shells. Bringing up the rear of the flotilla were the ironclad *Osage* and the timberclad *Lexington*, with the former strapped to the transport *Black Hawk*, a temporary relationship designed to keep the ironclad afloat. *Lexington* managed to open fire on the Confederates and *Rob Roy* joined in the exchange with her four heavy Parrott guns mounted on her bow. A portion of the lst Missouri Union Artillery on *Emerald* also managed to get a few shots off against the irritating enemy effort.[92] In making the turn around a bend, *Osage* ran aground, a calamity that exposed the transport *Black Hawk* to Green's Confederates. *Black Hawk* took such devastating fire that 40 soldiers on her decks had to be evacuated into the safe confines of *Osage* on the east side of the river. It did not take long before all hands on *Black Hawk* followed suit. When Porter later examined the ship, he observed that "there was not a place six inches square not perforated by a bullet."[93] *Neosho*, which was also grounded, finally freed herself and steamed down the river, firing along the western shore as she went. *Fort Hindman* and *No. 13* also managed to pull free and shot canister into

---

91   *OR* 34, pt. 1, pp. 570-571. Thomas Green, a solid commander from Virginia who identified more with Texas than his native state, led a command of some 1,200 troops at Blair's Landing. His force included the under strength brigade of William Parsons, together with two untested regiments, the 23rd and 36th Texas Cavalry, and Capt. J. West's 2-gun battery. Anne J. Bailey, "Chasing Banks Out of Louisiana: Parsons' Texas Cavalry in the Red River Campaign," Civil *War Regiments*, Vol. 2, No. 3, p. 219.

92   *OR* 34, pt. 1, pp. 381, 570-571.

93   Porter, *Naval History*, p. 512.

the Confederate forces for a distance of two miles along the river. This odd engagement, which pitted Confederate cavalry and a couple of field pieces against Union ironclads, gunboats, and transports, raged with undiminished intensity for about two hours. In his official report of the Action, Thomas Selfridge noted that "The rebels fought with unusual pertinacity for over an hour, delivering the heaviest and most concentrated fire of musketry that I have ever witnessed."[94]

Lexington finally managed to silence Green's artillery with her 8-inch guns. Just prior to this, however, *Osage* had broken away from *Black Hawk* and drifted toward the bank near where the Confederates were massed. Using *Osage* as a shield, Selfridge brought one of his heavy guns to bear on the enemy and at a distance of 20 yards, fired a load of canister at an officer who was urging on his gunners with a fiery passion while conspicuously mounted on a white horse. After the smoke cleared, wrote Selfridge, [I] saw him no longer." The large shotgun-like blast decapitated the unfortunate soldier, who turned out to be Thomas Green himself, a loss the Confederates could ill afford.[95]

The action came finally ended around 6:00 p.m. when the growing darkness, coupled with the command confusion following Green's untimely demise, convinced the Confederates to withdraw into the woods. The Battle of Blair's Landing was over. Although the Federals estimated that from 200 to 500 enemy were killed and wounded, Rebel losses were actually very low. Federal losses were not reported, but were probably light as well.[96]

The fleet continued downriver toward Grand Ecore until around 1:00 a.m., when it anchored for the rest of the night. The frustrations and dangers encountered on the previous day began anew on the morning of April 13. The quartermaster's boat *John Warner* ran aground and delayed the progress of the fleet. Confederate Brig. Gen. St. John Liddell, following the movement of the fleet from the east side of the river, planted some field pieces on high ground and began firing into the narrow river choked with Union vessels. *Osage*, however, quickly poured her metal into Liddell's men and drove them off before any damage could be done to the stalled naval column. The unfortunate *Rob Roy* lost her rudder and had to be placed under tow by the transport *Clara Bell*.[97] Not all

94   *ORN* 26, p. 49.

95   Porter, *Naval History*, pp. 512-513;   Anne Bailey, "Thomas Green," in Davis, ed., *The Confederate General*, 3, p. 33.

96   *ORN* 26, pp. 49, 55; *OR* 34, pt. 1, pp. 172-204, 571, 633.

97   *OR* 34, pt. 1 p. 382.

of the vessels were free to move, however. *John Warner* resisted all attempts to liberate her from the river's sandy bottom. At daylight on the morning of the 14th, an exasperated Kilby Smith left the ironclad *Fort Hindman* behind with *John Warner* while ordering his army transports and gunboats ahead to Campti. The next day, *Fort Hindman* pulled her off the bar and together they proceeded down the river.[98] By April 15 the entire fleet was safely docked at Grand Ecore. Although not a pretty sight—one Union soldier wrote of the fleet's return, claiming that "the sides of some of the transports are half shot away, and their smoke-stacks look like huge pepper boxes"—the fleet had narrowly avoided capture and/or destruction up Red River. Its survival was due largely to Porter and Smith, who managed to keep their military composure while fighting their way to safety at Grand Ecore.[99]

After the Federal defeat at Pleasant Hill, Banks retreated with his exhausted and defeated army in the direction of Grand Ecore. The infantry arrived ahead of the fleet. Upon his arrival, Porter paid a visit to Banks' headquarters tent. For field conditions, he found it rather opulent. The general was robed in a fine dressing gown, velvet cap and comfortable slippers. He was reading Scott's Tactics, his usual nightly ritual. The general made it plain that he felt he had "won at Sabine Crossroads and that Pleasant Hill was just a withdrawing action." According to Banks, he had withdrawn his army because of the lack of water! The admiral informed the politician that if that were the case, his army while at Sabine Crossroads had been only six miles from a river of water. Porter left the general "under the delusion that he had won the battle of Mansfield, or Sabine Cross Roads, or whatever name that unfortunate affair was known by." Totally disgusted with this whimsical dreamer and his justification for defeat and retreat, the admiral wryly noted that Banks "should have read it [Scott's Tactics] before he went to Sabine Cross Roads."[100]

Despite the growing animosity between the two officers and the serious setbacks encountered on both land and water, they did discuss the possibility of resuming the move to Shreveport. Porter expressed confidence that the expected rise in the river would enable the joint forces to head for Shreveport a second time. Banks, in turn, assured Porter than he intended to make such an attempt. The expected rise in the water level did not materialize, however, and Banks

98 Ibid.

99 Pellet, Elias P., *History of the 114th Regiment, New York Volunteers* (Norwich, New York, 1866), p.222.

100 Porter, *Incidents*, pp. 235-236; Porter, *Naval History*, p. 517.

received word from Steele in Arkansas that his column would not make it to Louisiana in time to support him.[101] In addition, Banks was being pressured by Grant and Sherman to return A. J. Smith's divisions to Vicksburg. Once again Banks was faced with an important decision. This time, he chose the right road and decided to retreat.[102]

On April 19 Banks ordered Smith to take his command and occupy Natchitoches for the purpose of covering the retreat. Smith reached Natchitoches the following day, and on the 21st at 5:00 p.m., the long and difficult withdrawal began.[103]

Porter and his fleet encountered difficulties from the outset. Prior to Banks' order to retreat, the admiral determined the river was falling so rapidly that the fleet had to withdraw quickly or risk being trapped. As a result, Porter moved his vessels down the river on April 16. Additional dangers awaited the ships. In mid-March, knowing that the fleet would have to return along the same river, Confederates placed six anchored mines below the ferry at Grand Ecore. *Eastport* was sent ahead of the fleet because of her great draft—she was the largest vessel in the fleet. The unlucky warship struck one of the torpedoes. According to Porter, the damage inflicted on the ironclad was slight, and "the shock only noticed by a few persons on board." The explosion may have been felt by only a "few," but the blast proved fatal and eventually sent *Eastport* to the bottom of Red River, although it took five hours before her keel imbedded itself in the shifting sand.[104] The *Eastport* obstacle was less threatening than the beached Southern *New Falls City*, but just as troublesome. The fleet was now bottled up behind her and she blocked its passage. If *Eastport* could not be removed from her watery resting place, the stationary fleet faced destruction in the narrow river channel.

S. L. Phelps, *Eastport's* commander, immediately heeded Porter's instructions and began lightening his vessel. He removed her heavy battery on the 16th, which was placed on flat rafts towed by *Cricket*, and utilized the pump boats *Champion No. 5* and *New Champion* over the next several days to remove the water from *Eastport*. "It would be tedious to detail the incessant toil of the

101   Steele's campaign came to grief because of bad roads, a lack of supplies and forage, harassing Confederate cavalry—and poor generalship. For more information on Steele's wing of the Red River Campaign, see Edwin C. Bearss, *Steele's Retreat From Camden and the Battle of Jenkins' Ferry* (Little Rock, 1967).

102   Winters, *Civil War in Louisiana*, p. 360.

103   *OR* 34 pt. 1, pp. 310, 428; ibid., pt. 3, p. 222.

104   Ibid., pt. 1, p. 505; *ORN* 26, p. 62.

people of my vessel day and night, assisted by parties from other vessels in the squadron," Phelps later reported. Phelps' laborious tasks continued unabated, and by April 21, his badly damaged gunboat was once again afloat—but just barely.[105]

Afloat, but still taking on water, she managed to travel downstream another 40 miles while carpenters from the different ships worked day and night to stop the influx of river water. Near the small town of Montgomery, the ill-starred gunboat ran into submerged snags and ground to a halt. The gallant pump boat *Champion No. 5* was again called upon for assistance, this time accompanied by her sister ship *Champion No. 3* and the tinclad *Fort Hindman*. All efforts to save *Eastport* proved fruitless despite the valiant efforts of Phelps and other members of the squadron. Porter, upon receipt of news that the water level was falling downstream, concluded that the fleet was in dire straits. *Eastport*, even though she was the most powerful ironclad in the Mississippi Squadron, had to be removed as an obstacle to the rest of the fleet. Porter ordered a ton of powder placed throughout the doomed vessel and at 1:45 p.m. on April 26, she was blown to pieces.[106]

As Porter progressed downriver with *Cricket* in the lead, it appeared that the worst was behind him. For 15 miles the vessels traveled without incident. The admiral's wishes notwithstanding, dangers still awaited his floating command. As he approached the mouth of the Cane River, he encountered a Confederate 4-gun battery under the command of Capt. Florian Cornay, bolstered by 200 riflemen from Maj. Gen. Camille de Polignac's division.[107] The Rebel guns heaped a destructive fire on the passing vessels. One Confederate shell penetrated *Champion No. 3's* boiler and sunk the ship, but not before the scalding steam escaping from the punctured iron tank killed more than 100 black contrabands jammed on board. *Juliet* and *Champion No. 5* were lashed together as they steamed past the deadly battery. Confederate fire struck the tiller ropes of *Juliet* and her steam pipes. Once the steam cleared, her captain discovered that both vessels were facing the wrong direction and that *Champion No. 5* was adrift and being abandoned by her crew. It appeared that both vessels were doomed. Had it not been for the heroic actions of William Maitland, one of *Juliet's* pilots, neither ship would have left the river. Maitland and part of his crew managed to

---

105   *ORN* 26, p. 78.

106   Ibid., pp. 72-77.

107   Ibid., pp. 74-75, 167, 169, 781-782, 786. Porter's report, ibid., p. 74, notes eighteen artillery pieces.

tie a line to the damaged vessel and *Juliet* hauled her upstream and out of immediate danger. Commander Phelps, who was put to piloting *Fort Hindman* after the unfortunate loss of *Eastport*, brought up the rear of the two vulnerable vessels.[108]

But danger was still ahead. Phelps and his men worked during the night to repair the worst damage suffered by *Juliet* and *Champion No. 5*. When all that could be done was completed, Phelps decided to run the battery and at 9:00 a.m. on April 27, *Fort Hindman*, with *Juliet* in tow and *Champion No. 5* following close behind, started downriver. Just before approaching the Confederate battery, *Juliet* hit a snag in the river that necessitated a withdrawal back upriver for repairs. Once these were completed, Phelps again tried to run past the battery. The vessels encountered heavy fire from the enemy and *Juliet's* upper works were hit hard and her machinery badly damaged. One shell passed through *Fort Hindman's* pilot house and destroyed the tiller ropes. Both vessels became unmanageable and drifted through the heavy Southern fire. Surprisingly, both also passed the battery still afloat. *Champion No. 5*, however, was not as fortunate. Lead and iron so badly damaged her that her crew abandoned the ship to the Confederates.[109]

The Cane River engagement proved to be quite costly to the navy. Two transports had been lost and three tinclads severely damaged. *Cricket* suffered 38 hits and 25 dead and wounded, fully one-half of her crew. *Juliet* also lost half her crew, with 15 killed and wounded. *Fort Hindman* lost even more.[110] Confederate casualties were but one wounded sharpshooter and one officer, Captain Cornay, who was killed. The Rebels, however, were not successful in stopping the Federal retreat.[111]

Upon his arrival in Alexandria, Admiral Porter faced yet another challenge—perhaps his most difficult of the entire arduous expedition. The river had fallen some six feet, and the fleet was bottled up above what he called the "Falls." Not only did the rapids have to be dealt with but the rocks below them, according to Porter, were "for a mile quite bare, with the exception of a channel twenty feet wide and three feet deep." Porter, on board *Cricket*, ordered her pilot to make the attempt to negotiate this channel and "after considerable thumping"

---

108 Ibid., pp. 74-75, 167, 169, 781-782, 786. Porter's report, ibid., p. 74, mentions eighteen artillery pieces.

109 *ORN* 26, pp. 82-84, 169, 176.

110 Ibid., p. 76.

111 Taylor, *Destruction and Reconstruction*, p. 218.

she passed the falls.[112] The transports and light-draft tinclads followed *Cricket* on her bumpy ride through the strait. Porter was elated his light-draft vessels were able to move beyond the rapids, but his jubilance was tempered by the knowledge that the pride of the entire Union inland navy was still stranded literally a stone's throw from freedom behind the falls. His numerous and powerful men-of-war—*Lexington*, *Fort Hindman*, *Osage*, *Neosho*, *Mound City*, *Louisville*, *Pittsburg*, *Chillicothe*, *Carondelet*, and *Ozark*—remained trapped. More than $2,000,000 worth of naval capital were at risk. If they fell intact into enemy hands, their use could alter the war on the inland waterways. But the admiral had few choices other than to wait for the river to rise.[113]

Banks' choices were likewise limited. Although he found Porter's fleet safely anchored at Alexandria, it could not move downriver until the water level increased. As a result, Banks' only viable alternative was to remain and defend Alexandria in order to shield the fleet from capture or destruction. Thankful for the army's presence, Porter was hopeful the fortifications being constructed around the city by Banks' embattled army would prove sufficient protection against Richard Taylor's approaching force to preserve his fleet until deeper water allowed his ships to slip away to freedom.[114]

Taylor was not about to rest on his laurels. He had inflicted a sharp defeat upon a superior force at Mansfield and came close to victory again the next day at Pleasant Hill. His subordinates had pestered the Federal navy at Blair's Landing and inflicted notable damage to the fleet at the mouth of Cane River. The Confederate commander had no intention of abandoning the initiative he had fought so hard to obtain. Indeed, he began to encircle Alexandria. As historian Ludwell Johnson described it, Taylor "proceeded to beleaguer 30,000 men with 6,000." The withdrawal of Banks and Porter left most of Louisiana west of the Mississippi under Confederate control.[115]

With forces already to the north of the town, Taylor sent a brigade of Brig. Gen. James P. Major's cavalry and J. A. A. West's battery 30 miles south of Alexandria to David's Ferry, not far from Marksville, a move designed to prevent Banks from communicating with Federal forces on the Mississippi

---

112 Porter, *Naval History*, p. 524.

113 *ORN* 26, p. 94.

114 *OR* 34, pt. 1, p. 310.

115 Johnson, *Red River Campaign*, p. 254. Even with his small numbers, Taylor exercised considerable control over what was once Union-held territory—even to the extent of enlisting recruits for Confederate service. Ibid., pp. 254-255; *OR* 34, pt. 1, pp. 585-586.

River. Another squadron of cavalry was sent to Simmesport and Fort De Russy. Brigadier General Liddell was wreaking havoc with Union infantry and naval forces at Pineville, opposite Alexandria, and the Federal garrison at Plaquemine was driven within its lines. Even the Bayou Teche region had been cleared of Federals, freeing W. G. Vincent's cavalry to move on Marksville and Simmesport. With the exception of Alexandria, which Banks had ringed with two lines of fortifications, Louisiana's parishes west of the Mississippi River were again under Confederate control.[116]

Those of Porter's transports and tinclads that had managed to float down the rapids received the initial onslaught that resulted from Taylor's encirclement tactics. On May 1, Major and West captured and burned the transport *Emma*, and two days later on May 3, *City Belle*, moving north to Alexandria with 700 men of the 120th Ohio on board, was likewise captured. More than 300 officers and men from the Ohio regiment were taken captive and a large number wounded and killed during the fighting.[117] On May 5, the Federals suffered a defeat greater than the earlier affair at Cane River when they lost *John Warner, Signal,* and *Covington.*[118] Including *Emma* and *City Belle*, Banks and Porter had lost three transports, two gunboats, and some 600 soldiers and sailors. As the campaign's historian aptly put it: "For the time being, at least, the Red River was closed to Federal shipping."[119]

While the Confederates pounded away at the Federal transports and gunboats southeast of Alexandria, Porter was nervously waiting for the river to rise so his ironclads could pass over the rapids to freedom. As it turned out, a natural rise in the river was not necessary to save Porter's fleet. Colonel Joseph Bailey, an engineer on the staff of Maj. Gen. William B. Franklin, had informed the general prior to the navy's ascent of the river that if the water was too low when the ships began their descent, he could remedy the problem by creating a series of wing dams, construction marvels that would artificially raise the water level and allow the fleet to cross the rapids. Facing precisely that predicament, Franklin, remembering his prior conversation with Bailey, called on him to address the problem at hand.[120]

116   *OR* 34, pt. 1, pp. 583-586, 635-636.
117   Ibid., pp. 475, 5 85-586; *ORN* 26, p. 102.
118   Ibid., 25, pp. 114, 119, 123, 134; *OR* 34, pt. 1, p. 442, 475, 621.
119   Johnson, *Red River Campaign*, p. 257.
120   Porter, *Naval History*, p. 525.

Born on May 6, 1825, in Ohio, Bailey studied civil engineering in Illinois before moving to Wisconsin to become a lumberman. He was mustered into the army on July 2, 1861, and served as captain of a company of the 4th Wisconsin Infantry. He spent most of the war under Benjamin Butler and Nathaniel Banks in the Department of the Gulf, where his knowledge of engineering was utilized with distinction during the difficult Port Hudson campaign and around New Orleans. At Alexandria, he was about to face his most difficult engineering challenge and earn even greater distinction.

After obtaining the approval of Banks and Porter—the latter was initially hesitant and did not believe the effort would work—Bailey commenced his arduous task during the first week of May. Many in both branches of the service were openly skeptical of the scheme and had little faith in its success. As a result, Bailey's dam became the source of jokes by both Federals and Confederates.[121] Several buildings in and near Alexandria were scrapped for materials, including the Louisiana Seminary of Learning and Military Academy in Pineville.[122] At times, 3,000 men worked day and night to complete the dam. While wood was being stripped from buildings and forests, every available forge was used to craft iron to bind the dam together.[123] By mid-afternoon on May 8, *Fort Hindman*, *Neosho* and *Osage* entered the rising waters provided by Bailey's ingenious structure, gathered speed, and successfully negotiated the rapids.[124] Early the next morning, *Lexington* followed suit, and by May 13 all of Porter's vessels were safely over the rapids. Bailey was the hero of the hour.[125]

During the next few days Porter's fleet passed safely by General Major's irksome battery, rounded Fort De Russy, floated by Simmesport and headed for the safety of the Mississippi River.[126] The admiral reached the mouth of Red River aboard *Cricket* and transferred via tug to his flagship *Black Hawk*. Waiting on board was Maj. Gen. Edward R. S. Canby, commanding officer of the Military Division of West Mississippi. Canby was sent by Henry Halleck to relieve Banks of his command. Writing to his mother on May 18, Porter joyfully

121   James Wilson, "The Red River Dam, With Comments on the Red River Campaign," in *Personal Recollections of the War of the Rebellion, Addresses Delivered before the New York Commandery of the Loyal Legion* (New York, 1891), p. 84.

122   Johnson, *Red River Campaign*, p. 261; *ORN* 26, pp. 130-131.

123   *OR* 34, pt. 1, pp. 585-586.

124   Ibid., pp. 209, 254; *ORN* 26, p. 131.

125   Ibid.

126   Kerby, *Kirby Smith's Confederacy*, p. 318.

noted: "I am clear of my troubles and my fleet is safe out in the broad Mississippi." In an impressive understatement, Porter wrote, "I have had a hard and anxious time of it."[127]

After Banks' army inflicted additional destruction on Alexandria, it abandoned the town on May 13 and marched toward Simmesport on the Atchafalaya River. In order to cover the withdrawal of Porter's ships, Banks marched his army along the south bank of Red River as far as Fort De Russy. Fortunately for the beleaguered political general, his divisions encountered only sporadic harassment along the way from various elements of Confederate cavalry. Three days out of Alexandria on the morning of May 16, Banks found Taylor's small army drawn up across his line of retreat near Mansura, on the prairie of Avoyelles. A four-hour artillery duel ensued before Taylor's Confederates withdrew from the field. Banks reached Simmesport the following morning, two days after the arrival of Porter's ships at that place. A sharp rearguard action was fought by a portion of Banks' army on May 18 at Yellow Bayou as the bulk of the Union force was constructing a bridge of steamboats across the Atchafalaya River. The spirited Union defense was successful, and on May 19-20, Banks' men crossed the bridge and marched toward the Mississippi River.[128]

Upon reaching the Mississippi, A. J. Smith's divisions headed north to join the Army of the Tennessee and, in the words of a private in Banks' army, "The Red River campaign was over and nothing left to show for it but the great waste of man and money it had cost." Porter was more blunt in his assessment of the campaign: "Thus ended the Navy's connection with the Red River expedition, the most disastrous one that was undertaken during the war."[129]

Many of the principals involved attempted to shift the responsibility for the campaign's failure to someone else's shoulders. As commander-in-chief, President Lincoln was ultimately responsible for the defeat along Red River, a campaign he supported largely for political reasons. Although he had but little faith in a successful outcome, one of the reasons he sanctioned the campaign was to please New England's cotton factors and manufacturing interests. Even Secretary of State William H. Seward, who desired a Union presence in Texas and convinced both Lincoln and Halleck that diplomatic gains would come from

---

127   *OR* 34, pt. 3, p. 491; David D. Porter Papers, Division of Manuscripts, Library of Congress.

128   *OR* 34, pt. 1, p. 193; Welcher, *The Union Army*, pp. 762-763.

129   Kerby, *Kirby Smith's Confederacy*, p. 318; Porter, *Naval History* p. 534.

a successful military venture in the Trans-Mississippi Theater, must share some of the responsibility for the defeat.

Virtually all of the chief military personnel behind the operation were culpable to some degree for the campaign's failure. General Halleck had played a key role in planning the campaign, insisting that the operation be conducted and designating the route it should take. Major General William T. Sherman convinced a reluctant Ulysses S. Grant that the campaign was necessary and would bring positive military results. In spite of his friendship with Sherman, Grant—especially after he became general-in-chief—should have either canceled the expedition outright or loosened the shackles that hamstrung Banks. The constraint regarding the early return of Smith's divisions to Mississippi, an almost impossible timetable given the circumstances Banks would likely face along Red River, would have been difficult for any commander to overcome.

Once the expedition began, a number of key mistakes directly led to its failure. Banks, not the best choice to lead the expedition in the first instance, took the wrong road at Grand Ecore and led his army inland, away from his own supply line and naval support toward Taylor's waiting Confederates and defeat at Mansfield. His decision to march his army inland is even more culpable since a reasonably good road paralleling the river was available. His failure to properly reconnoiter the local geography was inexcusable—especially with a dangerous army lurking nearby. Admiral Porter is also not without blame. He misjudged the usefulness and capabilities of his fleet on the narrow and treacherous Red River. His decision to spearhead his fleet at Alexandria with *Eastport*, his heaviest ironclad, was also questionable given the unpredictability of the waterway and warnings of his pilot. Her grounding and the consequent naval traffic jam were all foreseeable events that would not have occurred with proper planning.

*   *   *

By mid-May 1864, the Red River Campaign was over. It accomplished nothing but the loss of property and human lives. The seizure of cotton by Porter's men, without satisfactory reimbursement to the planters, antagonized that class and caused many to burn their crop rather than have it confiscated. Most important, however, the campaign may have delayed the end of the war a number of weeks by siphoning many thousands of troops away from Sherman, and by postponing the more decisive movement against Mobile, Alabama—the campaign General Grant had wanted all long.

Theodore P. Savas

A Death at Mansfield

Colonel James Hamilton Beard
and the Consolidated Crescent Regiment

*F*or Maj. Gen. Nathaniel Banks' defeated and demoralized Union soldiers, darkness was a long time coming on April 8, 1864. Bullets and Richard Taylor's triumphant Southerners followed them as they stumbled in retreat through tangled woods and across fallow fields, through patches of briar and over the bodies of their freshly killed comrades. As the contagion of defeat coursed through the Union army, accouterments once judged indispensable were strewn about in confusion, marking the path of its three-mile quest for sanctuary. Even weapons had become superfluous to many of the retiring Yankees. A bottleneck created by abandoned artillery pieces and wagons, many of which were broken and burning in the twilight, hampered those officers attempting to stem the downward spiral into anarchy. What had minutes before been a stubborn defense had quickly escalated into a rout of serious proportions, a fragmented rearward flood of defeat that continued to pour across the Louisiana countryside until fresh Union reinforcements and merciful darkness ended the decisive battle of Mansfield.

A handful of miles up the road at her family home at Kingston, a nervous Kate Beard anxiously awaited news of the fate of her husband, Col. James H. Beard, the commander of the Louisiana Consolidated Crescent Regiment. Unable to relax indoors, she spent part of her day beneath a tree outside her home listening to the deep-throated thunder of artillery and continuous roar of small arms fire, eavesdropping on the thousands of men killing and maiming one another less than twelve miles to the southwest.[1]

---

1 Beard Family History, Beard Family Papers. Copies of these family records are in the possession of Nancy B. Wilson, Kentfield, CA., a descendant of Edward "Ned" Beard.

Kate Beard was still awaiting word as to the fate of her husband when darkness drew its curtain over the torn Louisiana landscape and the clamorous din fitfully echoed away into an uneasy silence.

Although he is more commonly associated with Louisiana, James H. Beard came into life two states to the east in Lowndes County, Alabama. He was born on July 28, 1833, the first of seven children for Edward Derrel Beard and Caroline V. Rembert. His parents had married two years earlier in Orangeburg District, South Carolina, and at some point soon thereafter made the arduous several hundred mile trek west with a number of other local families to Lowndesboro, Alabama. James' six siblings—two brothers and four sisters—followed at fairly regular intervals. The last of Edward's and Caroline's offspring, Edward "Ned" Derrel Beard, was born on September 20, 1844, exactly one month to the day after the death of his father. The stress of losing a husband, especially when about to give birth, took its toll on Caroline. Her delivery, too, may have been a difficult one. She did not survive the year. Eleven-year old James, together with his half-dozen siblings, suddenly found themselves orphans.[2]

Virtually nothing is known of James' formative years, although his subsequent success in the business world and surviving bits of polished correspondence manifest more than a passing brush with education. He moved from Alabama to Red Bluff, Louisiana (on what is now the Caddo-DeSoto Parish line), in the early 1850s. The earliest record of his domicile in that state is an October 1854 lumber purchasing record from Thos. Jefferson & Co. Stearn Mill of DeSoto Parish. He found employment as a store manager in an dry goods establishment owned by Charles A. Edwards.

On September 30, 1857, James married Catherine E. Hoyle Tomkies of Kingston, Louisiana, an ostensibly fortunate choice since all surviving accounts suggest their matrimonial union was a happy one. Since it was not an unhappy marriage that drove him to a new career away from home, perhaps the drudgery of clerking dampened his ardor for the dry goods business. Whatever the case, not long after his marriage the newlywed was plying the Red and Mississippi

---

2 Genealogy of the James H. Beard Family, Beard Family Papers. Edward Derrel Beard's Last Will and Testament was probated in Wilcox County (just north of Lowndes County), Alabama. Family history has it that the Beard children were split up and raised by friends and relatives. Ned was taken in by E. C. Norris, who eventually resided in DeSoto Parish, Louisiana. James' exact fate after the death of his parents and before his abrupt appearance in Red Bluff, Louisiana, a decade later, is unknown. Family lore suggests that both parents perished in a cholera epidemic.

rivers as a steamboat captain, still under Edwards' employ. Apparently the river engagement did not suit the restless Beard either, for an 1858 advertisement in a local newspaper confirms his return to the world of dry goods in the form of Childers & Beard, a mercantile business at 200 Texas Street near the corner of Spring Street, just two blocks from Shreveport's bustling wharves.[3]

Conducting a business proved to be one of Beard's long suits, and he rapidly accumulated a substantial amount of wealth. According to the 1860 Census, the 27-year-old dry goods merchant owned a residence valued at $6,500 as well as personal property worth almost $30,000—a more than tidy sum for a young man in pre-war Louisiana. Providence also smiled on James and Kate as husband and wife. That same year on February 5 the first of two children , Corinne Gayle, was born.[4]

On New Year's Day 1861, several weeks before Louisiana passed its ordinance of secession, James raised and organized a company of volunteers from amongst the 2,500 citizens of Shreveport. He was elected the company's inaugural captain. According to one newspaper account written long after the war, the newly-minted captain's "Shreveport Greys" were "hastily improvised . . . unarmed, unequipped, unorganized [and] untrained, but they were ready to fight for the South.[5] Contemporary accounts confirm that the company, like most of its companion organizations cropping up throughout the Southern states, organized without satisfactory arms, equipment, or uniforms. Much to the pleasure of the members of the company, the latter were not long in arriving. William E. Moore, a citizen of Shreveport who would eventually become the company's last captain during the Civil War, noted in his journal on the 4th of January that he "Drilled in uniform for the first time in [his] life," although the exercise was conducted in private during evening hours. The evening drills may have increased the marching skills and consequently the confidence of the Greys, who four days later paraded before public eyes in broad daylight. The Greys celebrated the anniversary of the Battle of New Orleans, explained the

---

3   Ledger of Thos. Jefferson & Co. Steem (sic) Mill, 1851-1855, John F. Tomkies Papers, LSU Shreveport Archives, No. 294; unidentified and undated newspaper clipping, Beard Family Papers. The announcement described the establishment as a "new and spacious brick store." The future colonel was also a member of the Masons. He was "Raised to the sublime degree of a Master Mason in Jeffersonian Lodge No. 138 at Kingston, DeSoto Parish, La." on July 10, 1858. Masonic Document, Jeffersonian Lodge No. 138, Beard Family Papers.

4   Genealogy of the James H. Beard Family, Beard Family Papers.

5   Unidentified newspaper clipping, Thursday, – 11, 1936, Beard Family Papers.

obviously proud Louisiana private William Moore, "by drilling in public, the first time that I made my appearance in daylight with [a] uniform on."[6]

Determined to do his best to outfit his men, Captain Beard left Shreveport for Baton Rouge on January 12 with the intention of securing arms for his company. His brief sojourn in the state's capital was successful and he returned home eleven days later laden with 350 rifle-muskets. The months passed as Beard's citizen-soldiers drilled and digested the rudiments of military discipline. In early April 1861, after the Charleston batteries brought about the involuntary exchange of the banners that flew above Fort Sumter, the Shreveport Greys became the first company to leave Shreveport to join the Confederate army. The neophyte soldiers left their home on April 16 bound for New Orleans on board the steamer *Louis d'Or*, with Pensacola, Florida, as their final destination. The martial appearance and composure of Beard's men impressed a reporter from the local *Shreveport Weekly News* who turned out to witness their departure. "It is usual to characterise [sic] volunteers by the most flattering epithets, but the character of the material of the Greys is beyond all praise," gushed the excited newspaper scribe. In an awkward and poorly-phrased statement that may well have stung several male citizens still residing in Shreveport, the paper claimed: "The best citizens, the very best men of Shreveport—its gentlemen—make up the file of this company." The company commander was in line for high praise as well. "Capt. James H. Beard is worthy of his command, and will make his mark, or nature made a mistake when she marked the man. If the war lasts, we shall hear from James H. Beard, now captain."[7]

According to Moore, the departure of the 130-man company was undertaken "amidst the greatest excitement I ever saw. The day was fair and the men all determined, though their countenances sad." An editorial in the *Shreveport Daily News* echoed Moore's sentiment: "The levee was crowded with ladies, gentlemen, and children, anxious to have another look at the brave defenders of our rights. As the boat left the shore, the band of the Caddo Rifles struck up a very appropriate tune, 'The Girl I Left Behind Me,' and the cannon was made to belch forth its thundering sound." The new soldiers were greeted the next day with a seven-round salute at Alexandria, where Gov. Thomas

6   "Diary of Captain W. E. Moore, Last Captain of the 'Shreveport Greys,'" *Shreveport Journal*, January 6, 1930, hereafter cited as Moore diary.

7   Moore diary, January 12, 23, 1861; Untitled article dated January -, 1930, by George L. Woodward, *Shreveport Journal*. Woodward mistakenly claims that the name of the steamer transporting the company was *Champion*; *Shreveport Weekly News*, April 26, 1861.

Moore and his wife joined the men for at least part of their passage down the Red River. New Orleans was reached late on the afternoon of April 18, as the excitement of wartime travel began to wear off the new soldiers. We "walked four miles to the barracks," scribbled one tired diarist, who was more than mildly distressed with what he found there. The Greys' temporary housing was, as he put it, "such a place as decent men never had to submit to before." He would experience far worse before war's end.[8]

Beard's Shreveport company left the Crescent City for Mobile, Alabama, two days later aboard the steamer *Florida*. Reaching that place on April 21, the men set out on foot and, over the course of the next three days, marched some 45 miles east to Pollard, Florida, where they boarded a train for Pensacola on the afternoon of the 25th of April. Captain Beard's Shreveport Greys was but one of five companies journeying to Pensacola to complete the organization of the 1st Louisiana Regulars Infantry Regiment.[9] The balance of the companies slated for service with the regular regiment completed the recruiting process and reported for duty at Pensacola late that May. By May 30, however, all five volunteer companies, about 600 men, had new orders to depart immediately for Virginia. Abandoning the state for the unknown was apparently welcome news. "All jolly and glad that we are leaving Florida," Moore noted in his journal.[10]

The Shreveport Greys pulled into Richmond, Virginia, late on the evening of June 7 after a fitful nine-day journey punctuated by sleeplessness, a lack of food, and a harmless but rankling train derailment south of Montgomery, Alabama. Four days later the five volunteer companies were organized as the 1st Louisiana Infantry Battalion and placed under the command of Col. Charles

8   Moore diary, April 16, 17, 18, 1861; *Shreveport Weekly News*, April 26, 1861.

9   Moore diary, April 20 - 25, 1861; Arthur W. Bergeron, Jr., *Guide to Louisiana Confederate Military Units, 1861-1865* (Baton Rouge, 1989), p. 148. The 1st Louisiana Regular Infantry Regiment was organized in February 1861 as a portion of the Louisiana State Army. Its 860 men transferred to Confederate service on March 13, 1861. Only three companies, however, had completed the recruitment process by the time the regiment was ordered to report to Pensacola. As a result, five volunteer companies were ordered to that gulf coast city to complete the regiment's organization. In addition to the Shreveport Greys, these five companies included the Grivot Guards, Crescent Rifles, Orleans Cadets, and Louisiana Guards. Ibid., pp. 70, 148. James Beard's 16-year old brother, Edward "Ned" Beard, accompanied the Greys from Shreveport and enlisted in Company D as a private on April 20, 1861. Compiled Service Records of Edward D. Beard, National Archives.

10   Moore diary, May 30, 1861. As was the case with many officers during the war, Beard was accompanied by "Alonzo," a black servant from the Tomkies family. James H. Beard Letter, May 1, 1861, Beard Family Papers. The 1860 Census does not denote the presence of slaves in the Beard household in 1860. Alonzo remained with Beard for the balance of his Confederate service.

Didier Dreux. The 29-year old colonel, a prewar attorney and state legislator from New Orleans, had attended both Amherst College and Kentucky Military Institute before graduating from Transylvania University.[11]

The companies of the battalion were soon moved from Richmond to the army coagulating on the lower Virginia peninsula for the defense of Yorktown. The soldiers continued to improve their lot by drilling and preparing to meet their Union counterparts. On the evening of July 4, 1861, Colonel Dreux gathered together 100 infantry, a handful of cavalry, and a small howitzer and marched out of camp on what was essentially a reconnaissance to locate and ambush an enemy reportedly committing acts of vandalism in the surrounding countryside. The contingent of green soldiers returned the next day carrying Dreux's corpse, which had been pierced by a single minie ball when the opposing sides exchanged fire along the road leading to Newport News. Private Stephen Hackett, who was also killed in the skirmish, bears the dubious distinction of being the first member of Beard's company killed in combat. Dreux's untimely demise—he was the first Louisiana officer killed in the war—resulted in the promotion of the battalion's major, Nicholas Rightor, to lieutenant colonel. Five weeks later on August 15, James Beard was elevated up the command ladder to major, filling the vacancy created by Rightor's earlier promotion.[12]

11   Ibid., May 30-June 7, 1861. The battalion was a 12-month unit, Bergeron, *Louisiana Military Units*, p. 148; Robert K. Krick, *Lee's Colonels: A Biographical Register of the Field Officers of the Army of Northern Virginia* (Dayton, 1991), p. 123. According to one postwar account by a member of the 1st Louisiana Battalion, Dreux and the five companies made the trip to Montgomery and points north for an entirely different reason. As the tale goes, when the 1st Louisiana Regulars Infantry Regiment completed its recruitment and organization with Regular soldiers, the five volunteer companies were "told they were out of service. Captain Dreux could not see this arrangement, and he marched his men to Pensacola, gathered together a few box cars, and proceeded to Montgomery, then capital of the Confederate States," the other companies following "as best they could." After two days in the new Southern capital, the companies "took a freight train and proceeded to Richmond. On the road . . . the five companies were organized into a battalion and Charles Dreux was elected colonel." John K. Renaud, "The Romance of a Rich Young Man," in *Confederate Veteran*, 40 vols. (Nashville, 1923), vol. 31, pp. 256-257. Renaud's interesting tale conflicts with contemporary documentary evidence and contains conspicuous exaggerations.

12   Bergeron, *Louisiana Military Units*, p. 148; Compiled Service Record of James H. Beard, National Archives. Two detailed articles exist regarding the particulars of Colonel Dreux's final hours: Columbus H. Allen, "About the Death of Col. C. D. Dreux," *Confederate Veteran*, 15, p. 307, and Just M. Lamare, "Col. C. D. Dreux," *Confederate Veteran*, 30, pp. 20-24. For a series of reports and letters detailing Colonel Dreux's first (and last) skirmish, see U.S. War Department, *The War of the Rebellion: The Official Records of the Union and Confederate Armies*, 128 vols. (Washington, D.C., 1890-1901), series 1, vol. 2, pp. 188-189. Hereinafter cited as *OR*. All subsequent references are to series 1; Krick, *Lee's Colonels*, p. 49, lists Beard's date of promotion as August 16, 1861.

The only identified photograph of Beard was taken in Richmond, Virginia, shortly after this promotion. The portrait is one of a handsome and obviously vigorous young officer in a full double-breasted uniform, the collar fastidiously adorned with the single star denoting the rank of major. His hair was thick and dark, parted on the right and grown long on the sides, framing a wide forehead and strong nose. His most prominent feature, however, was his thick flowing mustache, centered over a pronounced but not unattractive dimple that cleaved a rather square chin.[13]

A few weeks before Beard's promotion, a dark rumor began making the rounds in Shreveport that Captain Beard, according to one member of the company, "neglected the Grays [sic], and [had] not endeavored to provide for their comfort, and a quantity of other stories equally as foolish." The disparaging remarks were said to have originated from within the ranks of the Shreveport Greys. Beard first learned of the loose-lipped slander when he received a letter from a friend informing him of the idle but potentially damaging gossip circulating hometown streets. It struck him deeply. A sympathetic company member recalled that the captain "read the letter to the company, and could not keep back the tears." His denials, however, did not kill the vicious whispers. The uproar over Beard's comportment as company commander grew to such scandalous proportions that the men of the company felt compelled to assemble for a meeting to discuss the unfounded remarks. On August 10, 1861, an open letter to the hometown newspaper, written by many members of the company, trashed the claims: "The absurdity of such talk is sufficient not to require a denial for if ever a man was in love with a company, Capt. Beard is with the Grays [sic]."

On July 21, as the first major battle of the Civil War raged across the undulating plains of Manassas, the Shreveport Greys exonerated their captain of any wrongdoing. "Capt. Beard is devoted to the interests of this company, has constantly its welfare at heart, and has a just appreciation of the honorable post he holds," recorded the company assemblage. "Be it Resolved . . . that we hereby cheerfully vindicate Capt. Beard from such rumors and bear testimony to his amiability as a gentlemen and officer." The source of the deleterious rumors was never ascertained.[14]

---

13   This albumen print is housed at the Mansfield State Commemorative Area, Louisiana Office of State Parks.

14   *Shreveport Daily News*, August 10, 19, 1861.

Mansfield State Commemorative Area

Major James Hamilton Beard

Other than the baseless denigration of Captain Beard and the brief bit of excitement created by the slaying of Colonel Dreux—whom Maj. Gen. Robert E. Lee described in a letter five days later as "a gallant and accomplished officer"—the battalion's first ten months of service were utterly uneventful. The semi-ersatz war dragged on as the Louisianans continued drilling and serving on picket duty. As the initial excitement surrounding the national schism drained away, the Beards grew weary of their familial separation. The few letters that exist during this period convey their great depth of mutual love and respect and accentuate the longing that parents endure when separated from their beloved offspring. On August 6, 1861, just days before James' promotion to major, Kate Beard composed a chatty missive about life in wartime Louisiana, ending it with a sentimental description of her attempts to get 18-month old Corinne to "write a letter to her papa." Corinne, wrote Kate, "seemed quite eager to begin and I guided her hand, and she would make about one letter and then jerk the pen away and ram it into the ink," an artful description that must have brought a melancholy smile to her papa's face. "Corinne is well," Kate explained in another bit of correspondence several days later, but "she calls every man she meets 'papa.'"

In the same letter Kate provided ample evidence of little Corinne's rapid maturation in her father's absence:

> Mary went to the kitchen just awhile ago, and she [Corinne] came running to me and said 'Mama, Mary gone.' She makes gestures equal to a Frenchman, draws her face up and wags her head about. You would hurt yourself laughing at her. I know well enough who she will love the best when you come home, for she takes a fancy for any man she sees. The poor little thing is downstairs now calling me; I did not answer her, and she said 'Mama gone.'[15]

Enclosed within Kate's note of August 17 was a small length of a child's ribbon tied around a lock of Corinne's hair, the whole wrapped around a piece of paper containing childish gibberish only her absent parent could truly appreciate. Perhaps these personal effects eased slightly the soldier's angst at long separation from his loved ones. There was little else to break the monotony. Rightor's 1st Louisiana Battalion continued to perform its tiresome tasks on Virginia's peninsula through the latter months of 1861 and into the war's second spring.[16]

The shooting war, however, was about to begin in earnest in the Eastern Theater. On March 17, 1862, Union Brig. Gen. Charles S. Hamilton's III Corps division quietly boarded transports for the journey from Alexandria, Virginia, to Fort Monroe, at the tip of Virginia's peninsula formed by the York and James rivers. Hamilton's brigades were the advance element of Maj. Gen. George B. McClellan's grand attempt to capture Richmond by moving up the water-bound

15   Bergeron, *Louisiana Military Units*, p. 148; Letters from Kate Beard to James Beard, August 6 and 17, 1861, in John F. Tomkies Papers, Louisiana State University at Shreveport. The "Mary" referred to in Kate Beard's letter was probably James' sister, Mary Jane Beard, born in 1835. She died, unmarried, in 1897. Genealogy of the James H. Beard Family, Beard Family Papers.

16   Kate Beard to James H. Beard, August 17, 1861. "I am sitting on the floor, and she [Corinne] is sitting by me trying to pick off a watermelon seed that has stuck to the bottom of her foot," Kate wrote at the end of her letter of August 17. "I'll just send the seed for you to look at," she promised. Kate kept her word. Corinne's curl of hair, the ribbon that held it, the small piece of paper exhibiting her early penmanship— "the lines are hers without any assistance," noted Kate—and the tiny watermelon seed that stuck to a little girl's foot more than 140 years ago, are housed in the Beard Family Papers.

neck of land from the environs of Yorktown. By early April, forward elements of McClellan's Army of the Potomac had reached the formidable Confederate fortifications erected east of Yorktown and along Warwick River. The 1st Louisiana Battalion was deployed in an earthen redoubt along the right center of the Confederate line near Lee's Mill when the Union army began probing the Rebel defenses on April 5.

One veteran described the strong position held by the Greys at Yorktown as "a small earthwork" in which they received their "baptism of fire" for two hours from a six-gun battery. For Major Beard and the majority of his Shreveport Greys, the light and bloodless (for them) engagement was their first taste of war. Unfortunately, no details of how they performed has been found. Just as active operations began heating up in southeastern Virginia, however, the one-year enlistment term of the companies making up the battalion expired. The seriousness of the pending Union threat was not lost on the Greys, who promptly agreed to remain with the army until the current crisis was resolved. As one Louisianan described it, on April 11, 1862, "Our discharges from service were issued us . . . but, to the credit of the men, they remained on the line until the eve of Gen. [Joseph E.] Johnston's retreat to Richmond." The brief history of the 1st Louisiana Battalion ended on May 1, 1862, "when the battalion, having determined upon an artillery organization, passed out of existence."[17]

According to Louisiana historian Arthur Bergeron, Major Beard's Company D Shreveport Greys was assigned to the 1st Louisiana Infantry Regiment (as Company H under the command of William E. Moore) on June 27, 1862. The Greys went on to perform stellar service in the war's Eastern Theater. Beard did not accompany his men. Fourteen days after the disbandment of the 1st Battalion he was assigned as one of the majors of Lt. Col. Jacob D. Shelley's 11th Louisiana Infantry Battalion, which organized at Monroe, Louisiana, on

17   William J. Miller, "The Grand Campaign: A Journal of Operations in the Peninsula Campaign, March 17-August 26, 1862," in William J. Miller, ed., *The Peninsula Campaign of 1862: Yorktown to the Seven Days*, 3 vols (Campbell, 1993), vol. 1, pp. 182, 183; Maj. Gen. John B. Magruder's report of the April 5, 1862, engagements is found in *OR* 11, pt. 1, pp. 403-404. The Louisianans were part of Maj. Gen. Lafayette McLaws' Division, Magruder's Army of the Peninsula. Although organizational records for this period are incomplete, they were probably operating with, or attached to, the brigade of Col. Thomas P. August (15th Virginia Infantry) during the April 5, 1862, skirmish at Lee's Mill. Ibid., pp. 403; pt. 3, p. 460; Krick, *Lee's Colonels*, p. 39; n.a., "First Volunteers From Louisiana," *Confederate Veteran*, 3, p. 146. Of the 545 men who served in the 1st battalion, only two (Colonel Druex and Private Hackett on July 2, 1861) lost their lives on the battlefield, while 16 others succumbed to disease. Bergeron, *Louisiana Military Units*, pp. 148-149. The new battery formed from the expired enlistees was led by the captain of Company A, Charles E. Fenner, and went on to perform solid service in the war's Western Theater.

May 14 with 580 men divided into six companies. Shelley's Battalion remained in north central Louisiana through the fall and early winter of that year, drilling and performing picket duty while the war raged in Virginia, Maryland, and Kentucky. Although the transfer west, which took him closer to home, may have been welcomed by Beard, he could not have been pleased with the circumstances that greeted him in his adopted home state. Like most sectors of the Trans-Mississippi Theater, Beard's new precinct suffered from a dearth of military supplies and ordnance, and his men were not as well fed or cared for as they had been in Florida or Virginia. Disease ran rampant as a variety of contagious disorders plagued the units assigned to the District of Western Louisiana. The situation was so bad that by September 1, 1862, a captain wrote President Jefferson Davis' aide-de-camp that "This force [the units assigned to that department] has a heavy sick list, and furnishes but 1,000 men for duty." The lack of arms also concerned the officer. "I am informed by officers stationed here that there are but 1,200 stand of effective arms in this department, chiefly shot-guns." Although Beard endured these doleful circumstances for more than six months, we know little about his role during this phase of the war for none of his personal correspondence from this period survives. During the last month of the year the battalion migrated south to Rosedale, 15 miles west of Union-held Baton Rouge. The battalion's presence was intended to protect the Bayou Grosse Tete region from enemy forays originating in Baton Rouge.[18]

Early 1863 brought about a small measure of solace to the Beard family when James traveled home to Kingston that February. Using the surviving correspondence as a gauge, his stay at "Auburnia" was a happy one. The brief reunion also brought about the conception of James' only son, Charlie Edward Beard, who would be born on November 27, 1863.[19]

The months of dreary service in Monroe, Richmond, and Rosedale ended in early 1863 when the 11th Battalion withdrew to the vicinity of Simmesport and

18   Bergeron, *Louisiana Military Units*, pp. 149,164; *OR* 15, p. 805. The units operating in this department, under the command of Brig. Gen. Albert Gallatin Blanchard, were all from Louisiana (except for some Texas units and a Mississippi battery in southern Louisiana) and included two infantry regiments (28th & 31st), Shelley's Battalion, the 13th Battalion Partisan Rangers, R. G. Harper's company of cavalry (partisan rangers), and a four-gun light artillery battery. Ibid. For an interesting biographical sketch of General Blanchard, who carved his own niche as one of the most pathetic field commanders commissioned into Confederate service, see Arthur W. Bergeron, Jr., "Albert Gallatin Blanchard," in William C. Davis, ed., *The Confederate General*, 6 vols. (Harrisburg, 1991), 1, pp. 104-105.

19   Beard Family Papers. Charlie Beard was named after James' mentor, Col. Charles A. Edwards.

Fort DeRussy, just west of where the Red River snakes and turns before making its convoluted link with the Mississippi River. When Maj. Gen. Nathaniel P. Banks' Union forces moved directly against Alexandria in May 1863, the Louisianans rehearsed their role for the following year by retiring up Red River to Natchitoches, well into the state's interior. After joining Maj. Gen. Richard Taylor's small army shortly thereafter, the battalion moved into southern Louisiana that June, where Shelley's Battalion was attached to Brig. Gen. Alfred Mouton's Brigade. Thereafter, the battalion participated in the series of tedious marches and inconsequential skirmishes that occupied Mouton's Brigade through the remainder of the year.

Despite the proximity of the opposing forces, the generally lethargic posture assumed by the Unionists did not encourage any significant fighting during this period. Without steady combat thinning the officer corps, Beard enjoyed few opportunities for advancement. Despite the lack of serious fighting, an opportunity for promotion finally presented itself when Jacob Shelley, for reasons that remain obscure, resigned command of the battalion on August 3. Beard's promotion to lieutenant colonel was effective the same day. Unfortunately for the new battalion commander, the year drew to a close without the opportunity of leading his men in battle.[20]

A significant reorganization effected just before the close of the war's third year deposited Beard at the head of the regiment that would forever be associated with his name. Disease, desertions, and casualties had so dissipated the strength of many of Taylor's organizations that by the end of 1863, several of his battalions and regiments had shrunk to the size of two early-war companies—or less. In what would prove to be a successful attempt to remedy this vexing dilemma with three similarly-situated organizations, on November 3, 1863, Beard's 11th Battalion (about 300 effectives), together with the 12th Louisiana Battalion, were added to (or consolidated with) the Crescent (24th) Regiment. The resultant merger of these 14 companies at Simmesport, Louisiana, was tagged the Consolidated Crescent Regiment, and Beard was tapped to lead it as its colonel.[21]

A broader command reorganization took place later that month when Richard Taylor added an under strength brigade of Texans to his army and

---

20   Bergeron, *Louisiana Military Units*, pp. 164-165. The movements of Alfred Mouton's Brigade during the second half of 1863 are chronicled in Arthur W. Bergeron, "The Yellow Jackets: The 10th Louisiana Infantry Battalion," *Civil War Regiments: A Journal of the American Civil War* (1993), vol. 3, No. 2, pp. 1-30.

21   Bergeron, *Louisiana Military Units*, pp. 147, 164.

combined it with Alfred Mouton's Brigade to form a small division under Mouton's command. The new formation, grandly dubbed the "Second Division of the Trans-Mississippi Department," was headquartered in northern Louisiana in the Ouachita River country around Monroe. Although composed of solid fighting material, the field competency of its three high-level commanders was unsettled at best. Alfred Mouton, who had never officially led a division in action, was a native Louisianan of French ancestry and an prestigious 1850 alumnus of West Point (he graduated 38th out of 44 cadets). Although the Acadian had performed well at Shiloh at the head of a regiment, he later delivered two less than laudatory performances as an independent commander under the watchful (and critical) eye of Richard Taylor. Following these twin lapses, the major general damned Mouton's independent abilities with an odd mixture of commendation and faint praise: "While an excellent officer in the field, of great gallantry and fair qualifications, he is, I fear, unequal to the task of handling and disposing of any large body of troops." Although his personal bravery was beyond question, Mouton's lack of aggressiveness during several important weeks of operations at least hint at the possibility that Taylor may have been right: perhaps Mouton did not carry within him the natural instinct or ability to command large organizations in the field. His checkered military career certainly made his assignment as division commander something of a gamble.[22]

Mouton's brigade commanders were also question marks. Like Mouton, Taylor's selection to command the Texas brigade, Brig. Gen. Camille J. Prince de Polignac, was also risky. Polignac was a French aristocrat with limited military experience as a lieutenant in the Crimean War. Prior to his elevation to command the Lone Star regiments, the Frenchman's Civil War service consisted of staff assignments under P. G. T. Beauregard and Braxton Bragg, including a titular stint as flag bearer of the 5th Tennessee Infantry at the Battle of Richmond, Kentucky. Though something of a dandy, the handsome and polished scholar was reputed to be both a gambler and hard drinker. It was no small feat convincing the rough and tumble Texans to accept the self-styled "Lafayette of the Confederacy" as one of their own.[23]

---

22   T. Michael Parrish, *Richard Taylor, Soldier Prince of Dixie* (Chapel Hill, 1992), pp. 327-328; Taylor's quotation is taken from Bergeron, "Jean Jacques Alfred Alexander Mouton," *The Confederate General*, 4, pp. 192-193. Mouton's command failures took place in 1863 in southern Louisiana, where he failed to harass or otherwise disrupt occupying Union forces.

23   Terry L. Jones, "Camille Armand Jules Marie, Prince de Polignac," *The Confederate General*, 5, pp. 41-43.

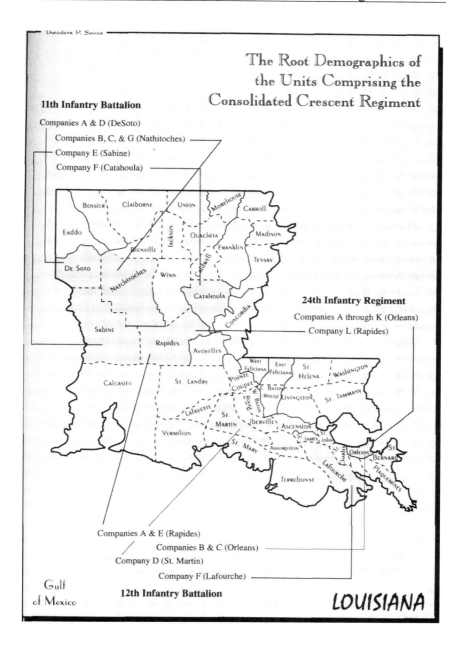

Theodore P. Savas

The Root Demographics of the Units Comprising the Consolidated Crescent Regiment

11th Infantry Battalion

Companies A & D (DeSoto)

Companies B, C, & G (Nathitoches)

Company E (Sabine)

Company F (Catahoula)

24th Infantry Regiment

Companies A through K (Orleans)

Company L (Rapides)

Companies A & E (Rapides)

Companies B & C (Orleans)

Company D (St. Martin)

Company F (Lafourche)

12th Infantry Battalion

Gulf of Mexico

LOUISIANA

Bossier · Claiborne · Union · Morehouse · Carroll · Eaddo · Ouachita · Madison · Jackson · Bienville · Franklin · De Soto · Natchitoches · Winn · Caldwell · Tensas · Catahoula · Concordia · Sabine · Rapides · Avoyelles · West Feliciana · East Feliciana · St. Helena · Washington · Pointe Coupee · W. Baton Rouge · E. Baton Rouge · Livingston · St. Tammany · Calcasieu · St. Landry · Lafayette · St. Martin · Iberville · Ascension · St. James · St. John · Vermilion · St. Mary · Assumption · Orleans · St. Bernard · Plaquemines · Lafourche · Terrebonne

Polignac's counterpart at brigade command, Col. Henry Gray of the 28th Louisiana Infantry, was less of an unknown to his subordinates (who included Beard) and the men in the ranks of his new brigade. Gray, who succeeded Mouton to the reins of the Louisiana Brigade, was a fiery native of South Carolina and prewar Louisiana attorney boasting no previous military experience before the Civil War. His forte proved to be training soldiers, a task he apparently relished. Gray's stellar debut at the head of his regiment in the April 12-13, 1863, Battle of Fort Bisland, coupled with a similarly competent performance two days later at Irish Bend branded him for future promotion. He would earn his collar wreath at Mansfield. James Beard's reaction to the promotion of Colonel Gray, as well as his relationship with him, went unrecorded.[24]

The first assignment of substance furnished Mouton's Division was the succoring of Confederates endeavoring to ship munitions west across the Mississippi River—weapons that Gen. Edmund Kirby Smith, commander of the Trans-Mississippi Department, considered vital to sustaining the war effort in the far west. The task proved much more difficult than it should have been. Poor communications and clumsy attempts at cooperation resulted in few arms actually passing over the waterway.[25]

After their stint as quasi-arms peddlers, Mouton's men spent much of the winter erecting defenses along the Ouachita River. This assignment was in anticipation of the opening of the 1864 spring campaign in Louisiana. Although senior military officers of the Trans-Mississippi Department were reasonably confident that Federal forces would attempt a major thrust up the Red River valley, there was an outside chance that a Union drive into the state's interior parishes would be made along the Ouachita. As a result, Mouton was ordered to move his division south along the river to the vicinity of Harrisonburg, Louisiana, a major road junction twenty-five miles northwest of Natchez,

---

24   Parrish, *Richard Taylor*, pp. 327-328; Bergeron, "Henry Gray," *The Confederate General*, 3, pp. 26-27; *OR* 26, pt. 2, p. 465. In addition to Beard's Crescent Regiment, Gray's [Mouton's] Louisiana Brigade consisted of the 18th and 28th Louisiana Infantry, 10th Louisiana Battalion, and Maj. Thomas A. Faries' Battery. After the reorganization, the November 10, 1863, divisional returns for Mouton's new command showed 220 officers and 2,654 men present for duty, the size of a single early-war brigade. This incomplete return, reprinted ibid., p. 465, states that Beard's old battalion was part of the brigade. By the time of the filed return, however, the battalion was no longer in existence.

25   William Arceneaux, *Acadian General: Alfred Mouton and the Civil War* (Lafayette, 1981), pp. 115-117. The clandestine nature of the arms shipments, coupled with the paucity of records for this period, make it impossible to definitively reconstruct the activities of Mouton's men.

Mississippi, where the Louisianans and Texans labored on defenses that would never be tested.[26]

The Consolidated Crescent's winter sojourn in northern Louisiana during the final weeks of 1863 and the first months of 1864 was perhaps the most difficult time endured during the war by Beard and his men. The winter was unseasonably cold, and many of the soldiers did not have boots or shoes to keep their feet warm. Insufficient supplies of poor quality food compounded their misery, and the men were forced to sleep on the cold ground without tents or any other form of shelter. Desertions were rampant while morale, mimicking the mercury, plummeted to new lows. Mouton's biographer went so far as to compare his subject's hardships in northern Louisiana with those suffered by George Washington's men almost ninety years earlier at Valley Forge. The analogy is imperfect, but the Louisianans did indeed suffer terribly.[27]

As the early months of 1864 slipped by, the weathervane of Federal activity continued pointing to an advance up Red River. Union troops were being withdrawn from enclaves in Texas and transferred to Louisiana. A move in force up that river valley seemed dictated by military logic. Despite the well known vagaries of the Red River, a decisive thrust up its twisting course offered a cornucopia of opportunities. It was the only river that pierced deep into Kirby Smith's department with the capacity to accommodate both wooden and ironclad gunboats. Coincidentally, by 1864 western Louisiana was the only section of that state worth the price (in blood and treasure) of invasion. In addition to acting as a conduit for troops and supplies for a subsequent strike into Texas, the Red River valley played host to bulging warehouses, factories, machine shops, and three important cities: Alexandria, Natchitoches, and Shreveport. The rich valley was also stocked with tens of thousands of bales of raw cotton worth millions of dollars. The ease of the opening of a second Federal front below Little Rock, Arkansas, where Maj. Gen. Frederick Steele made his headquarters, was not lost on the Union high command in Washington. A foray in strength by Steele southwest against Shreveport would further divide the already-outnumbered Southerners and render an effectual Rebel defense of the region that much more difficult. Although masked in secrecy, Banks' plan to move up Red River was discovered in New Orleans by Richard Taylor's spies as

26   *OR* 34, pt. 2, p. 884.

27   *OR* 26, pt. 2, p. 465; 34, pt. 2, p. 842. See Arceneaux, *Alfred Mouton*, pp. 114-115, for a description of the winter hardships suffered by Mouton's Division during this period of the conflict.

early as the first week of March 1864. Even with this early confirmation of the pending invasion, the Confederates were unprepared to stop the maneuver when the ball opened the following week.[28]

By March 14, the combined Federal forces of Nathaniel Banks and Rear Adm. David D. Porter punctured the Confederate outer defensive shell by moving into Red River, occupying Simmesport, and easily capturing Fort DeRussy. With their eyes steadily fixed eighty-four miles upriver on the grand prize of Shreveport, the Union forces tramped and steamed their way upriver to Alexandria by March 16. This deep penetration by thousands of men, supported by Porter's powerful flotilla, made it apparent to the Confederates that Red River—and not the Ouachita River line—was the primary objective of the campaign into Louisiana. That consideration settled, Mouton's Division, still encamped at Lecompte on March 13, was ordered forward to Yellow Bayou to be in a position to support Maj. Gen. John G. Walker's Texas Division. Generals Taylor and Kirby Smith, meanwhile, struggled to concentrate all available forces to defend the vulnerable river route. As departmental commander, Smith called up a cavalry division from Texas and two small infantry divisions from Arkansas to bolster Taylor's puny force. Despite these and other frenetic exertions, by the first of April Taylor was able to field only some 8,000 bayonets to confront Banks, whose combined forces numbered nearly three times that figure.[29]

Light skirmishing ushered the vanguard of the Federal army into Louisiana. Without much difficulty, the head of the blue column drove 55 miles northwest up Red River and poured into Natchitoches on April 2-3. During the Federal juggernaut's easy march tentacles of indecision gripped Kirby Smith. The Trans-Mississippi's commander impounded Thomas Churchill's division in Shreveport while he pondered whether to send it on to Taylor or return it to Arkansas to confront Steele, whose Federals had by now occupied Arkadelphia. Steele's column, the real wild card in the campaign as far as the Rebels were concerned, posed a menacing threat from the north. While Taylor pleaded for

---

28   Robert K. Kirby, *Kirby Smith's Confederacy: The Trans-Mississippi South, 1863-1865* (New York, 1972), p. 283.

29   *OR* 34, pt. 1, p. 491; pt. 2, p. 1046; Arceneaux, *Alfred Mouton*, p. 126. Smith's reinforcements included a motley assemblage of cavalry regiments and battalions under the command of Brig. Gen. Thomas Green, and the infantry divisions of Brig. Gen. Mosby M. Parsons and Brig. Gen. James A. Tappan, both of which were under the command of Brig. Gen. Thomas J. Churchill. See also, Frank J. Welcher, *The Union Army, 1861-1865. Organization and Operations, Volume 2: The Western Theater* (Bloomington, 1993), pp. 749-765, for one of the best summaries of Federal operations in the Red River Campaign.

additional soldiers, he berated his superior's sundered strategic policy in a letter to Brig. Gen. William R. Boggs, Smith's chief of staff. "Like the man who has admitted the robber into his bed chamber instead of resisting him at the door, our defense will be embarrassed by the cries of wives and children," lamented Taylor as Banks drove ever deeper into the Louisiana heartland. In a parting stab at Smith, whom he despised (the feeling was mutual), Taylor cut right to the quick: "Action, prompt, vigorous action, is required. While we are deliberating, the enemy is marching. King James lost three kingdoms for a mass. We may lose three states without a battle." Public protestations and private seething notwithstanding, Churchill's thousands remained in Shreveport, and Taylor had little choice other than to continue retreating.[30]

Colonel Beard's Crescent Regiment, together with Mouton's other units, spent Saturday, April 2, camped on the Natchitoches Road about 1 ½ miles below Pleasant Hill. According to a member of Colonel Gray's staff, Walker's Texas Division camped with Mouton's brigades and was "scattered all around us." The proximity of the advancing Union army, now only fifteen miles away and drawing nearer as each hour passed, caused widespread speculation among the stationary Confederates. "The actual position of our troops and the fact that the enemy [is] advancing . . . indicate[s] clearly that our generals are disposed to put up a fight of some kind at this point," surmised staff officer Felix Poche. Although noontime cannonading in the direction of the enemy seemed to confirm Poche's suspicions, orders to retire ten miles in the direction of Mansfield were received late that evening.

Beard's Consolidated Crescent, together with the balance of Mouton's men and Walker's infantry, broke camp and marched all night until 7:00 a.m. the following morning. The fatiguing journey was conducted under a surreal umbrella of choking smoke and pitch darkness, the result of an extensive fire burning in the pine woods bordering the road. The cause of the fire is unknown, although it may have been lit to illuminate the army's route through the region's narrow roads.[31]

Before the army moved out, Colonel Beard penned his last letter home from this bivouac below Pleasant Hill. It is a fascinating document on many levels. After having dinner with an elderly neighbor he knew in more peaceful times, the weary officer sat down and scratched out twenty-two sentences to Kate. He

---

30   Arceneaux, *Alfred Mouton*, p. 127; Parrish, *Richard Taylor*, p. 338; *OR* 34, pt. 1, p. 522.

31   Edwin C. Bearss, ed., *A Louisiana Confederate: Diary of Felix Pierre Poche* (Natchitoches, 1972), pp. 103-104.

entrusted the letter to "Fred," a family friend who served in his regiment. "We expect reinforcements to arrive in time to make a successful stand here," the colonel explained, confirming Poche's judgment that the army was about to offer Banks battle. "I do not have any fear of our being able to whip the scoundrels here," he confidently boasted, "having the advantage of a good position & the army wants a fight." [emphasis in original] Morale in the Crescent Regiment, and indeed, throughout Taylor's army, was high. "The best of spirits pervades the entire army and no demoralization is produced by our falling back," he assured added.[32]

Other matters beyond purely military concerns occupied Beard's thoughts that early spring evening. Despite his confident guarantee to Kate that they would "whip the scoundrels," the personal consequences of a Confederate defeat below Mansfield loomed large in his last letter home. How could they not? Kate, Corinne and Charlie, some of his extended family and neighbors, and his beloved Auburnia, his family home, were only a dozen miles away and directly in the path of Banks' roaming Federals. "If we [Taylor's Confederate army] have to fall back towards Shreveport from here," he informed his wife, "tell your Pa that it is my advice for him to send off all of his negro men and such women as Lucy. I am so glad that there is a prospect of our going no higher [up river] than this. It would disturb me so much to be forced to retreat and leave you behind." [emphasis in original][33]

The concluding brace of sentences—"Kiss the children for me and give love to all the family. Goodbye Darling and may God bless and protect you and my little ones"—epitomize the poignant sadness that surrounds the final days of James H. Beard and his family. Even though he and his men had been campaigning within a few days' march of Kingston, his words confirm that he did not know his four-month old son, Charlie Edward Beard, had died five days earlier. James' use of the word "goodbye" is also of interest. In not one of his surviving wartime letters does he conclude with a word suggesting so much finality. Although there is no direct evidence to support a conclusion that Beard

---

32 James Beard to Kate Beard, April 2, 1864, Beard Family Papers. The colonel recorded in this letter that he gave Fred permission "to go down to see his parents for a few days." With the enemy drawing near and the potential of a major battle erupting at any time, it is odd that Beard would grant leave to anyone in his under strength command. The fact that he did so gives rise to reasonable speculation that Beard deliberately sent the young man out of harm's way.

33 Ibid.

had a premonition of his own approaching mortality, the context in which the word was used was, especially for Beard, atypical.[34]

After a relatively restful day on April 3, Taylor's army continued its withdrawal in the direction of Shreveport early the following morning. The winding gray and brown ranks twisted through Mansfield, the county seat of DeSoto Parish—"an ugly little town situated in the pine forest on a rather high hill," noted diarist Poche—before going into camp about five miles north of that place. Beard pitched his tent that evening along a peaceful stream only a few miles from Kingston and family. Once settled, the colonel put his men through additional drilling exercises that included the formation of a mock line of battle and the discharge of blank cartridges at an imaginary foe. One member of the Consolidated Crescent remembered that the retreats, coupled with the drilling and preparation for battle, made many of the men "wonder if we are going to have a fight this time."[35]

While Richard Taylor's army was enjoying a well-deserved respite on April 5, Nathaniel Banks' forces reached Grand Ecore, where the main road to Shreveport turned west—away from Red River and the critical sustenance and heavy metal support provided by Porter's powerful flotilla. There was an uncharted road hugging the stream, but Banks' refusal to conduct a proper reconnaissance left it untraveled. On April 6, the politician in a general's uniform confidently tugged the bit in his animal's mouth and pulled its head to the west, distancing himself from his dominant floating artillery arm. Ludwell Johnson, perhaps the campaign's most prominent operational historian, labeled this decision for what it was: "the turning point in the campaign."[36]

While Banks sat at Grand Ecore and pondered choices made unattractive by his own incompetence, Taylor suspended his retreat. Three reinforcing arms of converging Confederates were coalescing to deliver a blow against the invaders. The divisions of Mouton and Walker, which had been together for several days, were joined by a Texas cavalry column under Brig. Gen. Thomas Green near

---

34   Ibid. The words "Went in the morning" are carved on Charlie E. Beard's tombstone. He is buried in Evergreen Cemetery, Kingston.

35   Poche, *A Louisiana Confederate*, p. 104; Louis Hall letter to the editor of *Mansfield Enterprise*, March 14, 1910, in Beard Family Papers. Despite a lack of documentary evidence, it is possible that Beard visited his family at some point during the army's April 5-7 sojourn above Mansfield. His camp was only a few minutes ride by horseback from Auburnia. If so, he would have learned at that time of his son's death.

36   Ludwell H. Johnson, *Red River Campaign: Politics and Cotton in the Civil War* (Baltimore, 1958), p. 115, See ibid., pp. 113-116, for a general discussion of Banks' decision-making process at Grand Ecore.

Mansfield, an important road junction thirty-five miles southwest of Shreveport. The third leg of the Rebel troika came about courtesy of Union general Frederick Steele. Harassed by Confederate cavalry and a lack of supplies and forage, Steele marked time in Arkansas instead of driving south to pressure Shreveport from above. His passivity finally convinced Kirby Smith to release Thomas Churchill's 4,000 infantry to Taylor's custody. The days of retreat along Red River had reached an end.[37]

As Confederate defensive preparations moved forward, Banks played into Taylor's hands by continuing his drive into the interior of Louisiana. On April 7, his cavalry met stiffening resistance a few miles north of Pleasant Hill at Wilson's Farm. Banks recklessly slogged forward, pushing his army in the direction of Mansfield. The mounted opposition was the recently arrived cavalry under Tom Green, which delivered a stinging but militarily empty punch at Wilson's Farm before withdrawing several miles to the rear. After the skirmish ended, the fiery Southern cavalry commander turned to one of his colonels and announced, "We haven't had much show yet, but we will give them hell tomorrow." Green's off-hand remark would prove remarkably prescient.[38]

At 2:00 a.m. on the morning of April 8, directives trickled down through the Confederate hierarchy ordering the army to begin marching south on the road to Pleasant Hill. With the exception of the ammunition wagons and ambulances, the balance of the trains were ordered to follow behind the infantry. This conspicuous omen "showed clearly that some action is contemplated today," scribbled Felix Poche in his journal. Beard's Consolidated Crescent, together with the balance of Colonel Gray's Louisiana regiments, did not begin its trek to the chosen field of battle until 6:30 a.m. Gray's infantry—the 18th Consolidated, 28th Louisiana, and Beard's Crescent infantry—passed through Mansfield and arrived on the grounds of the Moss plantation later that morning. As Beard's companies were approaching the front line along the Mansfield-Pleasant Hill Road, an exchange of artillery shells agitated a number of mules drawing wagons, causing them to mill about in confusion amongst the newly-arriving infantry. The men continued their march, threading their way into the woods bordering the north (left) side of the main road, where they passed behind Capt. T. D. Nettles' Valverde (Texas) Artillery, which was unlimbered in front of the tree line with its flag planted another twenty yards in front of the guns. The Louisianans double-quicked through the periphery of pines and approached the

37   Parrish, *Richard Taylor*, pp. 334-339.

38   Ibid.

lower part of a large open field, where they arrayed themselves for battle just inside the expanse of trees. All told, Henry Gray's small brigade probably did not number more than 1,000 men at Mansfield. They would number far fewer by the end of the day.[39]

It was no accident that the pivotal battle of the Red River Campaign was fought three miles below Mansfield. Richard Taylor, whose excellent eye for battlefield terrain had been honed earlier in the war under the tutelage of Gen. Thomas J. Stonewall Jackson, had carefully chosen his battleground the previous day while returning from the evening cavalry fight at Wilson's Farm. The area possessed several significant advantages for the Southerners that Taylor moved to exploit. The general expended several hours during the morning of April 8 deploying his legions in a two-mile concave crescent straddling the Mansfield-Pleasant Hill Road (modern Highway 175). The curved Rebel battle line was formed in the fringe of a piney woods just north of the Sabine Cross Roads, a thoroughfare that bisected the Mansfield-Pleasant Hill Road and ran west to the Sabine River. South of Taylor's selected position was open farmland 800 yards deep and 1,200 yards wide, a large field that once sprouted golden wheat but now law fallow. The wide expanse of this uncultivated soil was divided relatively equally on either side of the Mansfield-Pleasant Hill Road, which ran from the northwest (Mansfield) to the southeast (Pleasant Hill). The field's southeastern boundary was marked by a modest tree-studded slope known locally as Honeycutt Hill, which was bisected by the main thoroughfare. For Taylor's purposes, it was a powerful and compact position—especially for defensive operations.[40]

When complete, Taylor's deployment was as follows: Brig. Gen. Hamilton Bee's two regiments of cavalry under Cols. Augustus Buchel and Alexander Terrell held the extreme right flank, with Walker's Texas Division, consisting of the three infantry brigades of Brig. Gens. William Scurry and Thomas Waul, and Col. Horace Randal (from right to left in that order) extending the line up to and across the Mansfield-Pleasant Hill Road. Alfred Mouton's two-brigade division was on Walker's immediate left, with Mouton's right flank resting near the north side of the Mansfield Road. The right-front of the Acadian's divisional battle line was held by Polignac's Brigade, while Gray's regiments were stationed on

39   Poche, *A Louisiana Confederate*, p. 105; *OR*, 34, pt, 1, p. 563.

40   *OR* 34, pt. 1, pp. 563-564; Parrish, *Richard Taylor*, p. 341; Alonzo H. Plummer, *Confederate Victory at Mansfield* (Mansfield, 1969), p. 19; Welcher, *The Union Army*, 2, p. 754. This battle is also known as Sabine Cross Roads.

Mouton's left-front. The entire divisional line was established on a slight ridge just inside the wood line. The extreme left of General Taylor's two-mile long line was held by Brig. Gen. James Major's cavalry, three brigades of dismounted horsemen commanded by Cols. Walter P. Lane, Arthur Bagby, and William G. Vincent. Colonel Terrell's cavalry regiment was later shifted to this sector from the far right to extend and strengthen Taylor's left flank. Colonel Xavier B. DeBray's 26th Texas Cavalry, which was initially held in reserve on the Mansfield Road, was later deployed across the road well in advance of the infantry. Several batteries of artillery bolstered this imposing position, though only a handful of Taylor's guns would play a significant role in the upcoming fight. With fewer than 9,000 men in line, Taylor waited for Nathaniel Banks to attack.[41]

As the right-flank regiment of Colonel Gray's Brigade, Beard's Consolidated Crescent was the link with Polignac's regiments on its immediate right. Next to the men of the Crescent and holding the center of Gray's line was the 18th Consolidated Regiment, while the 28th Louisiana anchored Gray's left flank. According to Felix Poche, about noon the entire brigade snaked to the left to afford troops to their right additional frontage. "Yankee cavalry numbering about five hundred, silently emerged from the woods, and coming very bravely toward out lines, were at first mistaken for our own men." None of the officers on the scene, including Mouton, recognized the identity of these horsemen until they were about 200 feet from Gray's concealed infantry. Ignoring military protocol, Mouton personally ordered the 18th Louisiana to fire into the approaching troopers. The volleys, according to one witness, dispersed the probing cavalry and "inspired much enthusiasm among our troops, and at Genl Mouton's request our Brigade gave three cheers for Louisiana, whose sons had let the first blood of the day."[42]

---

41 *OR* 34, pt. 1, pp. 563-564; J. E. Hewitt, "The Battle of Mansfield, La.," *Confederate Veteran*, 33, p. 172; Johnson, *Red River Campaign*, pp. 132-133; Parrish, *Richard Taylor*, p. 341; Plummer, *Confederate Victory at Mansfield*, p. 19; Welcher, *The Union Army*, 2, p. 754.

42 Poche, *A Louisiana Confederate*, p. 106; Parrish, *Richard Taylor*, pp. 342-343. The bloodied Union cavalry belonged to Col. Thomas J. Lucas' brigade. Welcher, *The Union Army*, 2, p. 755. The timing of any particular sequence of events on any battlefield is always a difficult proposition. According to Louis Hall, a private in the Consolidated Crescent, his regiment was just arriving on the field when the Union cavalry launched its failed probe against the 18th Louisiana's position. Hall Letter, March 14, 1910, Beard Family Papers. It is more likely, however, that Beard's regiment had been on scene for some time before the cavalry action began. See, for example, the contemporary musings of Poche, *A Louisiana Confederate*, pp. 105-106.

Not long after the repulse of the inquisitive horsemen, the vanguard of Banks' infantry and artillery arrived near Honeycutt Hill and deployed for battle. Taylor, not a man of great patience, grew increasingly agitated when the anticipated aggressive Union action failed to materialize. Hours passed, both sides warily eying the other across the open field. And then it dawned on Taylor that an opportunity was slipping from his grasp. Banks' army was stretched out like a lengthy blue snake on the narrow road leading from Pleasant Hill. Taylor decided to emulate his early-war mentor, Thomas J. "Stonewall" Jackson, and seize the initiative. The several hours-long confrontation had reached a critical juncture. In a burst of audacity seldom equaled in the annals of the Civil War, Taylor decided to attack the head of Banks' substantially larger army and destroy it, folding it back upon the outstretched body.[43]

While Taylor had been contemplating his limited options, the opposing sides had settled into the deadly business of skirmishing. The contingent of skirmishers from the Crescent Regiment consisted of Lt. Abram H. Thigpen's Company B, which moved forward into the field and took cover in a shallow creek branch meandering through the center of the cleared acreage. From that point, Thigpen's men, according to one source, "annoy[ed] the Federals considerably." Captain Cyrus E. Dickey's corpse provided mute testimony of the veracity of this claim. Dickey, a Union staff officer and the son of the Chief Justice of the Supreme Court of Illinois, was shot from his horse by "Laffite," a Louisiana private hunkering down in the shallow ravine next to Lieutenant Thigpen. The intermittent firing punctuated with discharges of artillery occupied the early afternoon hours. Beard's remaining companies, lying prone close to the fence bordering the woods, suffered several casualties during this prolonged exchange. Private Louis Hall remembered that the "bullets [were] hitting the trees behind us, and now and then one of our boys would cry out from a wound."[44]

About 3:30 p.m., as the skirmishing along Mouton's front began to increase in intensity, Taylor arrived on horseback and greeted the Acadian and his subordinates. "Little Frenchman, I am going to fight Banks here, if he has a million men!" exaggerated the commanding general to Camille Polignac. "Let us charge them right in the face and throw them into the valley." After a brief

---

43   Parrish, *Richard Taylor*, pp. 342-343; Welcher, *The Union Army*, 2, p. 755.

44   J. E. Hewitt, *Shreveport Times*, April 5, 1925. Hewitt claims "Major [Captain] Dickey . . . was the first man killed in the battle of Mansfield," an interesting but unsupportable assertion; *OR* 34, pt. 1, p. 267; Hall Letter, March 14, 1910, Beard Family Papers.

conference with Mouton, Taylor ordered him to open forthwith the assault on the enemy in his front. His plan was to begin the attack with his left and continue the assault, en echelon, from left to right, thereby overwhelming Banks. Taylor may have spoken directly to Colonel Beard during his mid-afternoon visit to the Confederate left. Private Hall remembered that "an officer, I was later told it was Gen. Taylor, rode up to Col. Beard, and after a hasty conversation, Col. Beard ordered us forward." Whether Taylor conferred with the Louisiana colonel or not, after issuing his orders to Mouton he rode back toward the Mansfield Road, calmly puffed a cigar, and waited for the assault to begin.[45]

Delivering a properly coordinated *en echelon* attack is a difficult maneuver to pull off, but Taylor's late afternoon onslaught unfolded without any significant complications. Shortly after 4:00 p.m., Alfred Mouton's two brigades stepped over the fence that divided the barren field from the cover of woods, arranged themselves into a lengthy line at least two ranks deep, and moved against the Union army waiting less than one-half mile distant behind a stout split rail fence. According to one of Colonel Gray's staff officers, Polignac's Texans and Gray's Louisianans "with resounding yells . . . began running and stormed the enemy." By all accounts the offensive was impressively delivered. Taylor, whose military career—not to mention the fate of Louisiana and much of the Trans-Mississippi Theater—was riding on the points of Mouton's bayonets, recorded in his report of the battle that "the charge made by Mouton across the open was magnificent. . . . The field was crossed under a murderous fire of artillery and musketry, the wood was reached, and our little line sprang with a yell on the foe."[46]

As the Acadian's two brigades drove toward the right-center of Banks' Union line, the cavalry holding the left flank of Taylor's army joined in the sweeping assault. The advance of James Major's dismounted horsemen

45   *OR* 34, pt. 1, pp. 563-564; Parrish, *Richard Taylor*, pp. 343-344; Hall Letter, March 14,1910, Beard Family Papers. It is interesting to note that Private Hall did not recognize his own commanding general by sight. A postwar source claims that Mouton ordered Gray's Louisiana Brigade forward to prevent Captain Thigpen's company from being captured, and that the larger movement evolved into the attack that routed Banks' army. Hewitt, *Shreveport Times*, April 5, 1925. This theory is directly contradicted by Taylor's own report, and given the evolution of the battle, makes little sense. *OR* 34, pt. 1, p. 564.

46   Poche, *A Louisiana Confederate*, pp. 106-107; *OR* 34, pt. 1, p. 564. Union colonel William Landram, whose division sat opposite Mouton's brigades, placed the time of the Confederate assault at a precise 3:30 p.m. Ibid., p. 291; see also, John Minot Stanyan, *History of the Eighth Regiment, New Hampshire Volunteers* (Concord, 1892), pp, 402-403, which provides a good description ("no less than four lines in depth") of the weightiness of the attacking Rebel lines.

protected the left flank of Mouton's infantry as they sprinted across the uncultivated acres. After Mouton's and Major's men moved out, the jump-off point for the assault shifted to the right into John Walker's jurisdiction, where his patient Texas infantry were resting near the Mansfield road. With most of the army to his left charging ahead, Walker threw his three brigades, from left to right, into the developing metal maelstrom. Horace Randal's brigade, aligned on the left of the road, moved out first, with the brigades of Waul and Scurry following shortly thereafter. Brigadier General Bee, whose cavalry anchored Taylor's extreme right flank, also joined in the attack upon Banks' embattled vanguard. A description of the scope of the coordinated Rebel attack was recorded by one Federal soldier who wrote that "their lines extended so far that I could not see the ends on either flank."[47]

Richard Taylor later characterized the injurious reception his men received in the uncovered field as "a murderous fire of artillery and musketry." While accurate, the men who waded into this salutation of iron and lead surely deemed Taylor's précis to be an understatement of what they endured. Although the sudden and powerful attack developed quickly and fell across Banks' front like a rushing wave, the open field provided virtually no cover for the attacking Southerners. As a result, the bulging sickle of Union rifle and artillery fire harvested hundreds of Confederates in a manner not unlike that which befell the stalks of wheat that previously populated their avenue of approach.

Together with the other seven regiments of the division, Colonel Beard guided his Consolidated Crescent infantry from horseback that afternoon across the bloody field and into the pages of Louisiana lore. Accompanying him was his brother Ned Beard, who was serving on his staff. Mouton's two-brigade spearhead of Taylor's assault moved directly against Col. William J. Landram's Union division. As a result, it suffered disproportionately higher casualties than other Confederate units at Mansfield. "The Federals were strongly posted and reserved their fire for closer range," penned the editor of the *Mansfield Enterprise*. "The Crescent struck the enemy first and at close range received a volley from the 130th Illinois regiment that killed 55 men, including every field officer of the regiment, and wounded 150."

Felix Poche's vivid eyewitness account confirms the delivery of the close range musket volley. "At a distance of one hundred fifty feet the enemy opened

47   *OR* 34, pt. 1, p. 564; Poche, *A Louisiana Confederate*, p. 107; Stanyan, *History of the Eighth New Hampshire*, p. 412. The 8th New Hampshire (Mounted) Infantry, Col. Nathan M. Dudley's brigade, was stationed on the left flank of Banks' army.

fire and we were severely battered by musket fire and a really terrific cannonade," he testified, "the balls . . . crashing about us whistled terribly and plowed into the ground and beat our soldiers down even as a storm tears down the trees of a forest." A firsthand account by another Louisiana private recalled that he and his comrades jumped over the rail fencing and into danger at the double-quick, "firing as we went, our boys began to fall as soon as we cleared the fence."

These vivid descriptions of the carnage suffered by Mouton's men in general, and the Consolidated Crescent in particular, are supported by a Union soldier's graphically-drafted portrait of the same fateful charge. While the terrible fire was ripping apart the attacking lines, one member of the 96th Ohio Infantry (Col. Joseph Vance's brigade, Landram's division), remembered: "Shots plow gaps through them, shells burst in their midst and form caverns in the mass of living men, [but others] taking the places of their dead comrades, march rapidly on."[48]

A vivid postwar account in the *Shreveport Times* records the action on the front of the Crescent Regiment immediately following the close and deadly Union volley:

> This dreadful shock staggered this gallant regiment, man after man grabbed the falling colors and tried to bear them inward, only to fall as fast as they took it. Six had fallen, including the gallant Capt. Robert Seth Fields, of New Orleans, when the peerless regiment, without colors and with few officers, rushed forward, forced the lines of Federals, barricaded behind piles of rails, overwhelmed and . . . threw into confusion the whole Federal line.
>
> The cost was terrible, for the 130th Illinois was a typical regiment of American farmers who did not shoot and run away, but stood up manfully, realizing that they had the key to the situation and that victory or defeat depended upon their being able to hold their position.[49]

48 Hewitt, *Shreveport Times*, April 5, 1925; Poche, *A Louisiana Confederate*, p. 107; Hall Letter, March 14, 1910; Joseph Thatcher Woods, *Service in the Ninety-Sixth Ohio Volunteers* (Toledo, 1874), p. 59.

49 Hewitt, *Shreveport Times*, April 5, 1925. The "Capt. Robert Seth Fields" mentioned above was actually Seth R. Field, commander of Company A, Consolidated Crescent Regiment. Bergeron, *Louisiana Military Units*, p. 146.

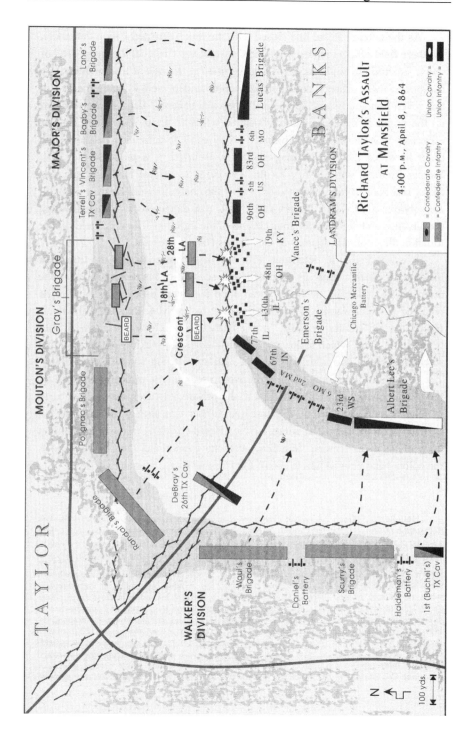

As the tattered Rebel line closed with the fence-shielded Union defenders, the Consolidated Crescent's field officers—each of whom entered the battle mounted—began to succumb to the hail of lead and iron. In addition to these officers, three company commanders were killed in the assault, and seven standard bearers fell beneath their silk banners. Felix Poche summed up the plight of the regiment at Mansfield when he wrote, "The Crescent, especially, was literally torn to pieces." Among the dead was Colonel James H. Beard.

One obscure but excellent account by Rebel J. A. Jarratt, a member of the Consolidated regiment, claimed "the first volley killed Colonel Beard and mortally wounded Colonel [Franklin H.] Clack. Major Canfield was not struck." Clack died shortly after the end of the fighting. Jarratt claims that Canfield dismounted, picked up the fallen regimental colors, ordered his men forward, and was killed by the next Union volley. According to Private Hall, however, Canfield was shot from his horse shortly after the charge began. It is impossible to reconcile these accounts. [50]

The ubiquitous Louis Hall found Beard's corpse shortly after he fell. "I had not gone far, before Maj. Canfield fell," reminisced the old soldier in 1910, "and I immediately afterwards tumbled, shot through the knee, which shook me up considerable." Seeking shelter from the screaming shells and whizzing bullets, Hall spied a log some distance away. The wounded soldier dragged himself over to soak up the protection offered by the tree. Unbeknownst to the private, however, the thin space behind the horizontal timber was already taken. As Hall crawled upon the scene, he witnessed Ned Beard clutching in his arms the limp body of his older brother. In a heart-wrenching emotional display, Ned shook the colonel and begged him to speak, but Corinne's papa was already dead. [51]

---

50   Hall Letter, March 14, 1910; Bergeron, *Louisiana Military Units*, pp. 146-147. The Consolidated Crescent was the only Louisiana regiment to lose all three of its field officers in a single battle (Mansfield) during the Civil War. Ibid. J. A. Jarratt, *Reminiscences of a Great Struggle by Heroes of the Confederacy* (privately printed, 1907).

51   Hall Letter, March 14, 1910. Like many of his subordinate officers, Alfred Mouton did not survive the attack. Although accounts of his death vary, he was probably killed while approaching a small knot of temporarily unarmed Union prisoners. The Acadian was riding in their direction when they picked up their dropped weapons and shot him out of his saddle at close range. There are several reports of atrocities committed upon Mouton's killers by a group of Louisianans who witnessed his death. Parrish, *Richard Taylor*, pp. 346-347n, states that the Yankees, "noticing his high rank" picked up their weapons and killed him. Arceneaux, *Alfred Mouton*, p. 132, repeats a quote from Gov. Henry W. Allen (who professed to being a witness to the charge at Mansfield) claiming Mouton was killed after trying to prevent his own men from firing upon unarmed Federals. Two other sources claim Mouton was killed during active combat. Poche, *A Louisiana Confederate*, p. 107, holds that Mouton met his death "while he alone was routing some fifteen Yankees." Poche's

Epilogue

Richard Taylor's coordinated assault resulted in one of the most spectacular Confederate victories of the war. His brigades reached and collapsed Nathaniel Banks' defensive position and drove his men pell-mell from the field. For the political general from Massachusetts, Mansfield would forever linger, the embarrassing defeat that marked the nadir of a spectacularly abysmal military career. For Taylor, the combat brought about the desired field victory and what he hoped would be the beginning of the end of the Union invasion up Red River. He was gravely disappointed. The following day at Pleasant Hill, Taylor's repeated hammer strikes were not nearly as coordinated or well-delivered, and the exhausted Union defenders managed, just barely, to fend off what almost evolved into a second catastrophic defeat deep within the interior of a hostile state. Ironically, both commanders viewed the Pleasant Hill fighting as a defeat. Banks, despite outnumbering Taylor about two to one, continued his demoralizing withdrawal to the relative safety of his gunboats. Although Taylor continued to harass the retreating Federals, his exhausted army, much reduced in numbers, could not prevent their escape from Louisiana.[52]

Ned Beard was not at Pleasant Hill. After the fighting, he commandeered a wagon and placed his brother's corpse in back before setting out for "Auburnia." Alonzo, James Beard's longtime personal servant, faithfully accompanied the colonel's remains home. The distance from Mansfield to Kingston was only about a dozen miles, but to the wagon's living occupants the journey felt ten times as long. The improvised hearse probably reached Kingston early on the morning of April 9. No records survive recording Kate's reaction to her husband's death or how she and Corinne coped with the sudden loss of one so dear. As the body was prepared for burial that morning, a packet containing a

---

account also implies that the general's death took place after the Union lines had been reached, which contradicts several popular accounts that Mouton died early in the fighting. Similarly, Hewitt, *Shreveport Times*, April 5,1925, grandly claims that Mouton died from an enemy volley after placing "himself at the head of the leaderless but furiously fighting Crescent." Neither Richard Taylor, in his report in *OR* 34, pt. 1, pp. 560-572, nor Ludwell Johnson, *Red River Campaign*, mention the circumstances surrounding Mouton's death.

52   Despite the fact that four decades have passed since the debut of Ludwell Johnson's *Red River Campaign*, it remains the best full-length treatment of the critical spring fighting in Louisiana, and thus must be consulted by anyone interested in this campaign. The discovery of previously-unknown manuscript materials, coupled with the ever-increasing interest in the war west of the Mississippi River, has amplified the need for an updated study of this important campaign.

small baby shoe belonging to one of his children was discovered inside the colonel's jacket.[53]

The family sent out small handwritten invitations to neighbors and loved ones announcing the colonel's hasty funeral. "The remains of Col. James H. Beard will be buried at Evergreen Church at 2 o'clock this evening," read the simple April 9 statement. Because only a few hours intervened between its arrival at "Auburnia" and burial at Evergreen Church, it is doubtful Beard's remains were embalmed. The internment took place as planned in the quiet little cemetery a few miles down the road, where he was laid to rest next to the fresh grave of the infant son he may never have seen. The outpouring of sympathy and praise for the fallen soldier and his family was as immediate as it was heartfelt. "As an officer, Colonel Beard enjoyed the trust and confidence of his superiors in rank and was honored and beloved alike by officers and men," eulogized a local newspaper shortly after the battle. Other newspapers echoed these sentiments. "As a citizen he ever stood high in the estimation of all who knew him. In all of the relations of life, he was without reproach."[54]

Kate, now a 28-year-old widow, had lost both her husband and her infant son within a span of less than two weeks. She never remarried. After the war she dedicated her remaining years to Corinne and the memory of the Confederacy. One source characterized her as "a woman with a purpose, she devoted herself to the activities of home and the loving bringing up of her little daughter." Auburnia, was described as "a refuge for the heart-weary and always a happy meeting place for the members of her family and her friends." Her contributions after the Civil War to the Daughters of the Confederacy were legion, and in appreciation of her efforts in this quarter, the organization formed the Kate Beard Chapter of the U.D.C. of Mansfield, which is still in existence today.

Kate's habitual "errands of love [and] mercy," as noted in an obituary, came to a sudden halt when a tragic fall confined her to a wheelchair for the final handful of her eighty-two years. She passed away at her home during the early evening of November 15, 1917—just a few weeks after other Americans began dying in another war.[55]

---

53   Bertha Beard Letter, April 14, [-], Beard Family Papers. Bertha Beard Brooke, Ned's granddaughter, resides in Los Gatos, CA. A brown leather baby shoe with a tiny heel and flower on the instep was found in 2002 at the Mansfield State Historic Site. It would have fit little Corinne when James left Shreveport for the front in early 1862.

54   Funeral notice, April 9, 1864, Beard Family Papers; n.d., n.a. newspaper article, ibid.

55   Unidentified newspaper obituary clippings, in Beard Family Papers. Corinne Gayle Beard married Robert Hall Scott on March 30, 1884.

Beard Family Portraits

Photos courtesy of Nancy B. Wilson, Kentfield, California

Catherine Tomkies Beard

This is the only surviving portrait of
James's beloved Kate, captured late in life.

Corinne Beard Scott

The grown daughter papa James never knew as a woman.

Edward "Ned" Derrel Beard

This is a handsome wartime photo of Ned, upon whose shoulders fell
the sad task of transporting his older brother's corpse home
to Auburnia in the back of a wagon following his
tragic death at Mansfield.

Auburnia, the home of James and Kate Beard, in a postwar view.

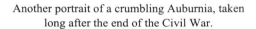

Another portrait of a crumbling Auburnia, taken
long after the end of the Civil War.

The obelisk erected at Mansfield in memory of the fallen James H. Beard, colonel, Louisiana Consolidated Crescent Regiment.

Edward Steers, editor

Occupation

Lt. Charles W. Kennedy and the
156th New York Volunteer Infantry in Alexandria

Someone once wrote that amateurs study strategy and tactics while professionals study logistics. While the merit of this statement is surely open to debate, it does highlight the fact that tactics and grand strategy usually attract most of the attention of readers of Civil War history, while issues of supply, logistics, and other similarly mundane duties are relegated to occasional articles in historical periodicals of limited circulation. Simply put, garrison duty and all that it encompassed—the construction of fortifications, the loading and unloading of supplies, and so forth—is not as exciting to read or write about as strategy and tactics, and yet was every bit as important to the outcome of the war.

The previously unpublished letters reprinted below supply intimate details on Union military life in occupied Alexandria, Louisiana, during the Red River Campaign of 1864. As the Federals moved out of that city and into the forbidding Louisiana countryside, Alexandria bustled with a frenetic level of military activity, all of which assisted, in one form or another, the important campaign being waged for the state of Louisiana.

The author of these invaluable letters is staff officer Lt. Charles Washington Kennedy, a member of Company I, 156th New York Volunteer Infantry. The 156th was organized at Kingston, New York, and mustered into service on November 17, 1862. The New Yorkers left their home state the following month for Louisiana, where they served mainly as garrison troops during the first several months of 1863. After a short stint in the trenches of Port Hudson in March of 1863, the regiment was sucked into operations against Richard Taylor's Confederates in western Louisiana, where they witnessed their first real combat at Fort Bisland on April 12-13. The men returned to Port Hudson during the last week of May and participated in the siege against that stronghold until its surrender on July 9, 1863. As a part of Brig. Gen. Cuvier Grover's Second

Division, the 156th New York spent the next nine months garrisoning the Louisiana capital of Baton Rouge before orders arrived calling on Grover to march his division to Alexandria as part of Maj. Gen. William B. Franklin's XIX Corps, where it would participate in Maj. Gen. Nathaniel P. Banks' attempt to capture Shreveport.

Lieutenant Kennedy's letters home to his wife Kate describe the hardships and toils of garrison life in an occupied enemy city. Few studies of the important Red River Campaign shed any light on this little-known aspect of the fighting in Louisiana. This fact alone makes Kennedy's letters especially valuable to students of the American Civil War.

*   *   *

As Grover's three brigades trooped into Alexandria on the morning of March 27, 1864, the vanguard of Banks' army—the contingent from the Army of the Tennessee under Brig. Gen. Andrew J. Smith—was marching out of the northern end of the city, leading the Union advance in its quest to subdue northwestern Louisiana. Since Grover's men were the last significant reinforcements to arrive in Alexandria, they were ordered to remain in that city as garrison troops. At the time of the occupation of Alexandria by Grover's division, Lieutenant Kennedy was serving on the brigade staff of Col. Jacob Sharpe, his friend and the former commander of the 156th New York.

*   *   *

Alexandria, La. HQ 3rd Brig 2nd Div 19th AC
March 27, 1864

My Dearest Katey,

In my last letter I said that I was afraid I would be unable to be as regular as usual in my weekly correspondence, but Sunday evening has come round once again and, though I am two or three-hundred miles away from where I was last Sunday, I am still in comfortable quarters and able to write to you as usual. I have had a very busy week of it. I had told you that we were in readiness to take the field on short notice. Well, on Tuesday last, the Adjutant General of our Division arrived at Baton Rouge with orders to send us off at once to Alexandria. You may perhaps recollect that Alexandria on the Red River was the farthest point to which we penetrated last Spring. It is between three and four hundred miles from New Orleans and about two hundred and sixty miles from Baton Rouge. The Steamer

Lt. Charles Washington Kennedy
156th NY Infantry

Courtesy of Edward Steers

Colonel Jacob Sharpe

Courtesy of Edward Steers

Lieutenant Colonel Alfred Neafie

Brevet Brigader Generals in Blue

on which the Adjutant arrived would only carry one regiment, so we put the 175th New York aboard, the smallest in the brigade, and started her off the same evening. Colonel Sharpe wished to send me ahead with the 175th to arrange matters for the Brigade, but I found it impossible to arrange my business so that I could leave. Our Quartermaster, Lieutenant [Albert] Mason, had been suffering from chills and fever but agreed to go in my place if I would undertake to manage his business as well as my own. This I had agreed to do and have done it, not only to his satisfaction and everyone else's, but to my own great astonishment now that I look back on it.

It was too much for any one man to undertake, but having undertaken it I was determined not to fail and I worked harder than I ever did in my life.

On Wednesday, I got off the 128th New York and the 38th Massachusetts. On Thursday, I worked hard all day from seven in the morning until six in the evening in a pouring rain shipping all the Brigade baggage and the wagon trains. I had over seventy mules to put on board and about twenty horses. All the wagons, twenty-one, had to be unloaded and taken to pieces, so you can imagine what a job it was to get them on board the steamer. Then I had to attend to my own business by shipping twenty wagon loads of provisions for the use of the Brigade. I can tell you I felt very happy when I was able to report, about six o'clock, that everything was safely aboard the steamer ready to start. As besides the freight, she would only carry about 200 men so Colonel Sharpe decided to put on board three companies of the 156th New York, the only remaining regiment, and to accompany them himself leaving the other seven companies to follow by the next boat. I was in hopes that he would allow me to stay to settle up my business with the Post commissary, but he said that he must have me with him as I had to leave one of my clerks instead. He kept the boat waiting an hour so that I could make the necessary arrangements to go with him. Of course it was a great deal pleasanter for me to be on the boat with him but I was afraid there might be some mistake in settling up the accounts if I was not there myself. Fortunately, however, there was no difficulty, and my clerk got here a day after me with my papers all correct.

We left Baton Rouge about eight o'clock on Thursday evening and we were at the mouth of the Red River (which runs into the Mississippi) about ten o'clock Friday morning. Alexandria is only a hundred and forty miles from the mouth of the river but the current is so strong and there are so many crooks and turns that we did not reach this place till day-break yesterday. We found General Banks here with nearly thirty thousand men, by far the largest army I have seen since I have been in the service. The town was full of soldiers, wagon trains loading up with supplies, officers and mounted orderlies galloping about in every direction, but the town itself looked just as Baton Rouge did when we first occupied it. Til the stores and houses were shut up and hardly one of the inhabitants to be seen in the streets. The 16th and 17th Army Corps marched out the day we arrived. They are Western men who came down the river from Vicksburg, good for fighting, but awfully rough. The inhabitants were in a sad state of tribulation while they remained here. They committed all sorts of outrages, ransacking stores and dwelling houses, and carrying off whatever they took a fancy to and destroying more than they took.

The first and third Divisions of our Corps are also here having come overland as we did last year. They leave here tomorrow morning. As soon as we arrived, General Banks detailed our Brigade to stay here and put Colonel Sharpe in command of the Post. This takes him away from the Brigade which is now commanded by Col. [James] Smith of the 128th New York. I felt very sorry about this although I knew it would not be for very long. Still, it broke up our family for the present, but Colonel Sharpe would not part with me and this morning I received a copy of a general order to this effect: "In addition to his duties as A.C.S. of the third Brigade, second Division, Lieutenant Charles W. Kennedy is appointed Aide-de-camp on the staff of the Post Commander. He will be obeyed and respected accordingly."

What do you think of that? I am now on the staff of two different commanders at the same time. The double duties will not last for very long. When Gen. Grover arrives with the rest of our Division he will . . . assume command of the town, which [he will] garrison, and then Colonel Sharpe comes back to the Brigade. The rest of the Army is going to Shreveport about 200 miles up river where the Rebs are in force, so we shall escape from a long and wearisome march.

I have got a first rate warehouse for my stores and for my quarters have had a nicely furnished room assigned to me by Lieutenant-Colonel [Alfred] Neafie of the 156th who is Provost Marshall of the town. My room is just as it was when the owner left it, everything in its place and a great deal more comfortable than even our quarters in Baton Rouge. Am I not lucky? Yesterday I worked hard all day getting my stores ashore and into the warehouse so I had no time to see about any quarters for myself so when night came I rolled myself in my blankets and lay down to sleep on the floor of the store, but alas it had been used as a flour and grain store and was full of mice who ran over me so that I did not get a bit of sleep. Do you recollect my telling you how the rats used to go into my bed on board ship? It is such a longtime ago that I have got out of the way of it and every time a mouse would run over me I had to jump and kick so that I got no rest at all. Tonight, however, I have a nice bed with clean white sheets (fancy?) and it does look so tempting that I don't know how I have managed to keep out of it long enough to write you such a lengthy epistle as this. It only wants one thing to make it all that I could desire . . . [undecipherable]. . . .

*   *   *

The river opposite Alexandria contains numerous rapids and shoals, and the unusually low water for that time of year prevented the unhindered passage of heavy transports past Alexandria. As a result, the transports were unloaded below the rapids and the cargo carried overland to a point immediately above the town, where it was reloaded onto the boats for passage upriver. This portage of supplies was delegated to Grover's 3rd Brigade, and became a principal responsibility of Lieutenant Kennedy's.

* * *

Alexandria, La. Thursday evening
March 31, 1864

Dearest Katey,

I wrote to you from this place last Sunday but as the mails are rather irregular, I do not like to let an opportunity pass without forwarding a letter. There is a man from the Brigade going to New Orleans tomorrow so I send this by him.

General Grover has arrived here with another Brigade of our Division and has assumed command of the Post. Colonel Sharpe is back again with his Brigade to everyone's satisfaction. The Army has all left with the exception of General Grover's Division, which is to hold this place. We will miss some hard fighting at Shreveport, but I suppose you will not grieve over that.

We are still in our comfortable quarters here enjoying the luxury of living in a furnished house and sleeping between sheets, but Grover, confound him, talks of putting our Brigade a little ways out of town, in which case we will have to go into tents which won't be very pleasant after living so long in a house.

I think we are likely to stay in this place for some time. I should not be surprised if it takes as long to capture Shreveport as it did Port Hudson. The people here say that it is very strongly fortified. Surgeons are getting the empty houses, of which there is no scarcity, fitting up as hospitals for the sick and wounded who are expected from the front. A lot of 62 came in yesterday who [were] wounded in a skirmish the day before only 12 or 15 miles from town, so it seems the Rebs mean to dispute every inch of the way from here to Shreveport.

General Banks with his Staff went up the river in a steamer this evening and now there is only our Division left here. I went out with a train of sixteen wagons and an escort of Cavalry the other day to get fuel for the Brigade. The passage of so large an Army has completely swept the country clean. There is nothing eatable to be had. Not a chicken or egg could we find. I did find two nice fat calves, however, which had somehow managed to escape. I had them killed and thrown on the wagons. We have lived on veal ever since. The owner looked very glum indeed when his calves were killed before his eyes without any leave asked, but he did not say anything. I did not feel the least compunction about taking Rebel veal without paying for it.

We have had no mail since we have been here and have no idea when we will get one. I am hungry for a letter. It seems a long time since I heard from you. I hope Wilbur called on you. I have written him a long letter tonight. If he should call on you on his way out again, it will be a good chance to forward anything you may wish to send to me.

Love to all the little ones and kisses from Papa and to yourself all that you know I feel for you. Goodbye Dearest Wife.

Your Own

Charley

*   *   *

Left behind to oversee the transporting of supplies around the rapids, Kennedy watched with some envy as Banks' army marched out of Alexandria toward Shreveport. He wrote to his wife that he would remain in Alexandria for a long time "unless our Army should be defeated."

*   *   *

Headquarters, 3rd Brig, 2nd Div. Alexandria, La.
April 3rd, 1864

Dear Katey,

I was afraid that my moving from Baton Rouge would interfere with the regularity of Sunday evening letters, but so far it has not—indeed I rather think you have gained a letter by the change, for I wrote once through the week fearing that something might prevent my doing so this evening. We begin already to feel at home in our new quarters. My duties are almost the same as at Baton Rouge and in a very short time we will fall into our old Post routine. General Grover is in command of the town, which is garrisoned by two Brigades of his Division. The regiments are posted so as to defend the town to the best advantage, and I understand that an extensive fort is to be built at once. Our Brigade is engaged in throwing up rifle pits in front of its position and everything looks as if our stay here might be protracted as it was at Baton Rouge. The regiments are encamped in small shelter tents, but they have built them up with boards so that they are nearly as comfortable as the large [tents] that they left behind. If we stay here for any length of time, we will probably send for the tents and regimental baggage.

General Grover is a very sensible man. His orders about going into tents referred only to the commanders of regiments, so the Brigade Commander and his Staff still continue to live in a civilized manner in comfortably furnished houses. The Quartermaster and myself still occupy the same rooms that we got when we first came. They are very comfortable and quite close to my warehouse which is convenient. The Colonel, his Adjutant and Aide, have quarters in a splendid house farther up town near the camp of the Brigade, but we all mess together in our quarters.

I have been working hard for two or three days past on my returns for last month and hope to get them off early next week. Every week seems to go faster than the one before it. Time seems to fly so that I can hardly realize that it is nearly six months since I left the regiment. Just think, we spent nearly one quarter of our three years quietly in Baton Rouge. It was nearly nine months since the fall of Port Hudson to the time we were ordered up here, and now we seem to be in for another long stay unless our Army should be defeated up at Shreveport and we should be forced to fall back. Don't you think that we are in luck to escape so much marching and fighting? But to tell you the truth, when I saw the Army marching out, with drums beating and flags flying, I would have given up all my chances of rest and comfort here to go along with it. It was a splendid sight, about thirty thousand men in splendid fighting condition fully equipped with everything necessary to make them efficient.

We have not had a mail since we came up here. It takes a steamer about four days to come up from New Orleans, and they are not at all regular. If we stay, I suppose that bye and bye we will be better off in this respect. At present, it is the only cause of my regretting leaving Baton Rouge. There we got our letters within a day or two of the steamers arrival at New Orleans. Now it will probably take as long to reach Alexandria from New Orleans as it takes them to get from New York to New Orleans. I suppose things are beginning to look a little spring-like in Cherry Lane. How I wish sometimes that I could just take a look in at you all if it was only for a minute, just to kiss you all around and see my little girl. I believe everyone you know here is well. Kiss my boys and baby for me. Think of me often and always as

Your loving husband,

Charles W. Kennedy

*   *   *

As the 3rd Brigade moved upriver from Alexandria, General Grover received the disheartening news of Banks' sharp defeat at Mansfield (Sabine Cross Roads) on April 8, followed by his strategic defeat the next day at Pleasant Hill. These twin setbacks, coupled with the failing river, which endangered Porter's fleet, changed overnight the entire complexion of the Union invasion of Louisiana. The besiegers suddenly became the besieged, as the initiative shifted to Richard Taylor and his victorious Southerners.

*   *   *

Alexandria, La.
Sunday, April 17th, 1864

My Dear Kate,

I have had a very busy week of it. Wednesday, I got orders to send one of I
have had a very busy week of it. On Wednesday, I got orders to send one of our
regiments up the river with ten days rations. The river is very shallow just above
the town so that all the stores, etc. have to be hauled about three miles further up
before they can be put aboard the boats. This makes a great deal of work.
However, I get along very well. The 38th Massachusetts was the regiment. I got
orders to move the remaining three regiments out to the landing and put them on
board the steamers that were waiting for them. It was two o'clock in the morning
before we got everything hauled out. To make matters worse, the night was dark
and rainy, and though I had three or four hundred men at work it was eight the
next morning before we got everything on board. I was completely worn out as I
had to do two men's work, the Quartermaster's and my own—Lieutenant Mason
not having returned from Baton Rouge. The boat on which I went carried the
156th New York, General Grover and his staff, and Colonel Sharpe and his Staff.
We were the last to start. We had only gone about fifty miles up the river when we
met a steamer coming down which hailed us and inquired if General Grover was
on board. On learning that he was, a dispatch bearer from General Banks came
alongside. There was a guard on the boat from the 38th Massachusetts and from
them we learned that when they were going up the river the day before they were
fired into with six of their men killed, among them a lieutenant son of their
Colonel.

As soon as General Grover read the dispatches, he ordered the boat to be put
about and away we went down the river again. We got back the same day and then
all the supplies had to be hauled from the landing back into town again. I tell you,
when I got through that night, I slept soundly. The regiments on the boats that had
gone ahead of us have not returned yet, but we expect them each day.

The Army has fought a great battle in which we suffered terribly, though we
finally drove the Rebs off. It has become very important, owing to the rivers
falling so rapidly, that this place [Alexandria] be held at all hazards and on this
account, we were sent back into the city. I should not be surprised if the Rebels
made a desperate effort to take it as it would compel General Banks to surrender,
being unable to get any supplies. Everything that comes in has to be unloaded
here, hauled up to the landing, and then reshipped. If they come, we will do our
best to keep them out as long as we can.

I have been relieved as Commissary and am busy closing up my accounts. I
have turned over all my stores and am acting as Quartermaster until Mason gets
back. After that, I don't know exactly what will be done with me. I expect to get
two months pay shortly after the first of next month and I will then send you as

much of it as I can spare. Write soon Darling and believe me to be With fondest love for you and the children.

Your Afft. husband

Charles W. Kennedy

*   *   *

On April 19, Banks issued orders for the army to return to Alexandria. Although Taylor made an all-out effort to stop Banks from crossing Cane River, his retreating army was able to brush aside the defenders at Monett's Ferry on April 23 and continue its retreat to Alexandria.

*   *   *

Alexandria, La.
Sunday evening, April 24th

My Dear Wife:

I am very tired and sleepy and can only write you a very short letter this time. Two hours ago I did not think that I would have a chance to write at all. We have been all packed up and on horseback ready to leave all the afternoon. I told you in my last letter about the battle that had been fought by General Banks in which we suffered and our being sent back when we were half-way up.

We occupied our old quarters quietly waiting for the arrival of the Army, which is falling back as fast as it can to this point, fighting all the way I am afraid. Today we received news that the enemy meant to attack General Banks at the crossing of a river about forty miles from here [Monett's Ferry on Cane River] and so we were ordered to march to his assistance. Just as we were ready to move, a courier came with dispatches to inform us that the Army had crossed in safety and that we need not go after all. I can't say that we felt very sorry. Things here look very squally and I fear that we will have a hard work to get back safely to some point that we are able to hold. This morning, the Rebel cavalry came down to the bank of the river opposite this place and fired a volley of musketry across at us, but a few shells from one of our gunboats soon drove them away.

The Army will probably reach Alexandria the day after tomorrow, but we cannot hold this place because of the river being so low that supplies could not get to us for any length of time. There is a large fleet of transports here which will probably carry the western troops up to Vicksburg and then we will have to take the back track towards New Orleans by land with the Rebs at our heels all the way. It is not a pleasant prospect, but we must make the best of it.

I have gotten out of the grocery business and have nearly finished settling up my accounts, but I still remain on the Staff. Colonel Sharpe does not mean for me to go back to the regiment for the present. I suppose that you have heard before this that Captain [Orville] Jewett has resigned and left the Regiment. I feel very sorry to have him go, but he could not avoid it owing to private affairs. No one feels so sorry about it as he does himself. I know all of the circumstances which led him to resign, and think that he could not have done otherwise.

And now I have a secret to tell you which you mustn't, for the present, mention to anyone. I am to be Captain of Company I. Colonel Sharpe has recommended me, and I will probably receive my commission as Captain in the course of six weeks or two months. That is, if we are spared to get out of this scrape we are in, as trust we will be. So you see, Dear Katey, that if nothing unforseen should occur, you will have to welcome me when I come home to you as a full fledged Captain, and Captain too of the only Company in the regiment of which I am desirous of being in command. But remember, not a word of this to anyone just yet.

Henry Buel's box came safely to hand the other day and I got my spectacles, stockings, cigars, and tobacco for which I owe you any number of kisses and thanks. The cigars were very good. I have not tried the stockings or tobacco yet, but mean to in the course of a day or two. Albert Heal and the other clerks are still in the commissary business with my successor, Captain [—] Darling.

And now my own dear wife, I must close with fondest love to you and the dear children. Write often and think of me always as

Your own

Charley

*   *   *

After his retreat to Alexandria, Banks found that the river had fallen more than six feet, which meant that Admiral Porter's fleet could not pass over the rapids at Alexandria and reach the Mississippi River. There was a very real possibility that the falling river would trap the Union fleet and render it virtually helpless against Taylor's approaching Confederates. Lieutenant Colonel Joseph Bailey, chief engineer on Maj. Gen. William B. Franklin's staff, proposed to raise the level of the river by constructing an elaborate arrangement of wing dams. Despite the doubts raised over the feasibility of this effort, the engineering feat successfully raised the river level more than six feet, and allowed Admiral Porter's deep-draft vessels to negotiate the falls and proceed down Red River to safety.

One incident of particular interest involved the 156th New York's commanding officer, Colonel Sharpe. On May 4, the transport *John Warner*, started out from Alexandria with an Ohio regiment aboard, convoyed by the wooden gunboats *Covington* and *Signal*. Shortly after starting out, *John Warner* was smothered by several volleys of musket fire. By the following morning, the Confederates appeared in force with artillery at Dunn's Bayou, approximately 40 miles below Alexandria. *John Warner* was disabled by Confederate fire and run aground. After sustaining a severe fire from the Confederate batteries while attempting to retreat upriver, *Covington*, followed by *Signal*, surrendered to the Confederates.

Some 250 and 300 officers and men were killed, wounded, or taken prisoner in the affair, Colonel Sharpe among them. From May 1 through May 5, five Union vessels (two gunboats and three transports) had been sunk or captured by the Confederate forces harassing the Union troops from both banks of the Red River. As Kennedy writes, Colonel Sharpe, though taken prisoner, escaped through the woods and made his way back to the regiment which was then encamped at Simmesport, Louisiana.

On May 11, General Banks marched his army out of Alexandria for Simmesport with the XIX Corps bringing up the rear. From Simmesport, the troops crossed the Atchafalaya river over a bridge of steamboats, ending the ill-fated campaign.

*   *   *

Morganza on the Mississippi
May 23rd, 1864

My Dearest Katey,

I suppose you have had a rather anxious spell about me. We have been cut off for some time from all communication with the outside world and have just managed to fight our way out. We got down to the Mississippi yesterday, and we felt as though we were once more at home. We have had so many exciting events, and have had such hard work to do since I last wrote, that I cannot recall exactly where I left off in my last account of our proceedings. Besides, the Rebels captured some of our mail boats on the Red River and probably some of my letters.

As soon as General Banks got back with his Army to Alexandria after his defeat, we went to work to build a dam in the river at that point in order to raise the level of the river so as to enable the gunboats to pass over the falls just above the city. It was truly a great undertaking for the river is very wide and rapid although quite shallow. The engineers, however, worked night and day and I am happy to say that the work was a success. We finally succeeded in getting the whole fleet over with the exception of one steamer [*Eastport*], which we were obliged to blow up. Meantime, the Rebs closed in all around us so that we could not go out more than a few miles in any direction without meeting them. Our Brigade went out on two or three expeditions in order to get forage for our animals, which resulted in two or three skirmishes in which we captured some prisoners. Our loss was only slight and nobody of your acquaintance was hurt. Up to this time the Red River was open so that we had communication with both the Mississippi and New Orleans, but the Rebs, who meant to gobble up the whole Army, planted batteries on the bank so that nothing could pass up and down the river. Thus we were completely out off from the rest of the world.

Before the river was closed, or rather before we were aware that it was, Colonel Sharpe received permission to go to Baton Rouge to see General [Philip St. George] Cooke, who was ordered north. He started out on a gunboat, which was going down as convoy for some transports. They had not gone more than forty miles down the river when the Rebel batteries opened on them and after a hard fight, with one gunboat sunk, captured the whole fleet. You can imagine our feelings when two days after Colonel Sharpe left, his colored servant made his appearance in a terrible plight having managed to get away when the boat was captured and made his way through the woods back to Alexandria. He told us that Colonel Sharpe was badly wounded and taken prisoner. You can imagine what a set of long faces there were on the staff when we got the news.

By this time, our supplies began to run short so that the men were put on two-thirds rations, but the dam was nearly completed with most of the gunboats over the falls so we got ready to leave. We left on the 11th of May and marched down the bank of the Red River, the gunboats and transports keeping abreast of the Army. We had to fight every day as we advanced, but the fighting was principally done by the cavalry who went ahead. When we got to the position that the Rebs had fortified and where they had captured our boats, we found that they had skedaddled. We than left the boats to make their own way down the river and marched crossed country to Simsport [sic] on the Atchafalaya. We had quite a fight on the way at a place called Mansura, but finally drove the Rebels back and got safely to Simsport. There, we crossed the Atchafalaya on a Bridge of steamboats and marched for the Mississippi, which we reached the day before yesterday. As to what is to become of us now or where we are to go, we are completely in the dark, but we shall probably not move again for some days. Men and horses are completely worn out and must have a rest. We have been marching and fighting every day and night since we left Alexandria.

There is a large fleet of transports here and we will be shipped to some point up or down the river. Vicksburg is talked about, but I hope we won't go there.

And now, Dear Katey, you know all about me. I am in first rate health and pretty good spirits although it makes me a little homesick to see people who have just come from home. But never mind. My turn will come some day. I have not yet received my pay nor my Captain's commission, but I expect they will both be along shortly. I forgot to tell you that Colonel Sharpe is back with us all right. He made his escape through the woods, and got on board a gunboat going to Baton Rouge. He joined us at Simsport. I am still on his Staff and likely to remain there. So the third Brigade has its Commanding officer back again. Wilbur says the baby is a perfect little picture. How I long to see her and all of you. Kiss them all for me and believe me to be as ever.

Your own,

Charley

*   *   *

Following the war, Charles Kennedy returned to his beloved Katey and their three children on Staten Island. On his return, he found his old job with Barrett, Nephews & Company waiting for him. As the years passed, he steadily rose within the corporate leadership, becoming vice president and treasurer of the prominent firm. He became a major figure in the civic community and was a leading force in establishing a county-wide system of public education.

Kennedy died in 1916 at the age of 83 in the same home from which he marched off to service fifty-four years earlier.

Gary D. Joiner

Driving Tour of the Red River Campaign

ost people interested in the Civil War develop a desire to visit the battlefields and sites associated with it. Although some battle sites are well marked, preserved in the public trust as park sites, and interpreted, many important sites remain unmarked or have disappeared forever in urban sprawl. Others remain inaccessible on private property and are difficult to find—especially because modern roads do not always follow historic routes. The fact that many campaigns stretched far and wide across the landscape only makes personal tours that much more difficult.

Anyone interested in tracking the spring 1864 Red River campaign in Louisiana will confront each of these issues. Several key sites still await interpretive signage. Only slivers of two of the campaign's primary battlefields (at Mansfield and Ft. DeRussy) are protected as park land. Every other battlefield and related site is under private or semi-public ownership.

The campaign was waged in an area roughly 160 miles long and 30 miles wide from Shreveport in the northwest to Simmesport in the southeast. (Shreveport was Banks's objective and a major logistical hub, but fighting never reached it.) This elongated rectangle is today dominated by four features: U.S. Interstate I-49, Louisiana Highway 1, U.S. Highway 71—and the Red River. The major cities in the campaign area are Shreveport, Natchitoches (pronounced náck-a-tish) and Alexandria. Several smaller municipalities are also of interest. These include Mansfield, Pleasant Hill, Robeline, Colfax, Boyce, Mansura, Marksville, and Simmesport. Each of these population centers were either battle sites or are the closest points from which to gain access to more remote areas of interest.

Most of the country roads in this region occupy the same roadbeds used in 1864, and much of the area is still rural. Other than a few minor changes, like the addition of a handful of residences and the occasional commercial structure, the land remains remarkably similar to what the Union and Confederates soldiers witnessed during the spring of 1864.

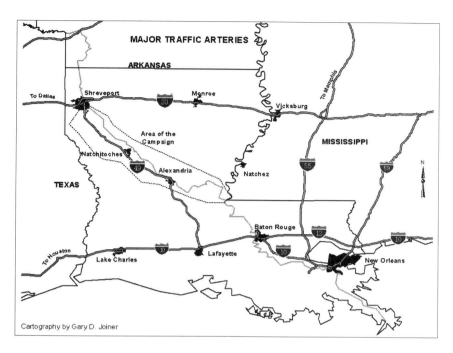

This brief tour guide article anticipates that you have both a working knowledge of the campaign (i.e., you have read this book) and that you have a road map of Louisiana. Therefore, this essay provides only general historical information about the sites mentioned herein. I also strongly encourage that you bring along maps of the primary battles. Because there is so much to see and space is limited, this article will focus on the following major sites of interest: Ft. DeRussy (March 13), Yellow Bayou (May 18), Mansura (May 16), Grand Ecore, Monett's Ferry (April 23), Wilson's Farm (April 7), Mansfield (April 8), Pleasant Hill (April 9), Blair's Landing (April 12).

Visitors from Baton Rouge and New Orleans will likely begin their study from Alexandria. Those arriving from points north, east, or west should probably begin their tour in Shreveport or Natchitoches.

For most of its length Louisiana Highway 1 bisects the campaign area. With few exceptions I-49 runs to the south of Louisiana Highway 1, the Red River runs parallel and just to the north of it, and U.S. Highway 71 runs parallel to and north of the Red River. Trips to battlefields will always begin from either I-49 or Louisiana Highway 1. Serious visitors should set aside three and possibly four days to drive to and fully examine all the sites of this campaign. Alexandria is the logical place to begin the first leg of the tour; Shreveport or Natchitoches are suitable for the final portion of the excursion.

Southern areas of the campaign offer a sense of traditional Acadian or "Cajun" culture. Most of the residents speak with an accent reminiscent of their French heritage, which has been prevalent in the region for over 250 years.

Fort DeRussy and the Battle of Yellow Bayou: The first part of the tour out of Alexandria runs through the Avoyelles Prairie to the confluence of the Red and Atchafalaya rivers. Admiral Porter brought his large fleet of 90 warships and transports into the Red River on March 12, 1864. The army under Brigadier General Andrew J. Smith was landed at Simmesport to trek overland for an attack against Fort DeRussy north of Marksville. This structure was the major Rebel defensive work on the lower Red River. Porter led his fleet up the river to assist the army. Some 300 Confederates defended the fort. Union forces attacked DeRussy on March 13 and captured it after a short fight. Simmesport was now a major Union base of supply. The area around Simmesport also saw the last action of the campaign at the Battle of Yellow Bayou on May 18, 1864.

The distance from Alexandria to Simmesport is approximately 70 miles. From Alexandria, take I-49 south approximately 30 miles to the Bunkie exit, (Exit 53) and turn left. Take the left fork at the exit ramp, which is Louisiana Highway 115. Drive approximately eight miles to the town of Bunkie. East of Bunkie this road turns into Louisiana Highway 29. After continuing on

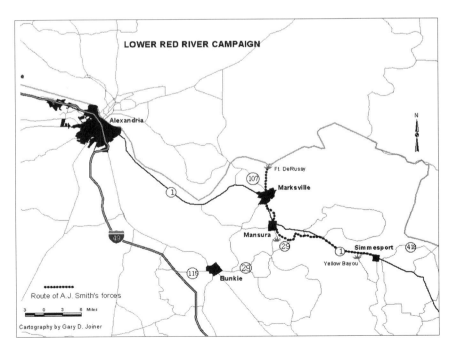

Louisiana Highway 29 for approximately 16 miles to Moreauville, turn right on Louisiana Highway 1 and proceed approximately 16 more miles to Simmesport.

You can cross the Atchafalaya River at Simmesport. The bridge there is located at the point where Colonel Joseph Bailey constructed a pontoon bridge (not to be confused with his wing dam) by lashing the Union army transports together side-by-side to allow Banks's army to evacuate the Red River Valley immediately following Yellow Bayou in May 1864. Turn around and drive back into town. Less than one-half mile east on Louisiana Highway 1 you will cross Yellow Bayou. Here, Union forces held back attacking Confederates long enough to allow the army to escape over Bailey's pontoon bridge. On the north side of Louisiana Highway 1 and south of Bayou de Glaize is a Louisiana State Park that is the site of one of the so-called "Yellow Bayou" forts.

From Simmesport drive northeast on Louisiana Highway 1 about 15 miles to the intersection of Louisiana Highway 1186. Turn left and travel another one and one-quarter miles to Louisiana Highway 114. Turn right on 114 and proceed a short distance to the town of Mansura. This small town gave its name to a battle fought on May 16, 1864, fought in the heart of the Avoyelles Prairie. Here, Confederates tried unsuccessfully to halt retreating Union forces. According to several accounts the battle was a magnificent artillery duel, though with very few casualties. These same accounts also describe the beauty of the land and the magnificent array of the armies.

The battlefield is triangular-shaped, with the town of Marksville at the upper end, Mansura along the eastern leg, and the town of Hessmer along the western leg. The bottom of the triangle is formed by Lake Pearl. You may circumnavigate the fighting area by taking Louisiana Highway 114 west from Mansura to Hessmer, Louisiana Highway 115 north to Marksville, and Louisiana Highway 1 back to Mansura, The entire circuit is less than 16 miles.

From Mansura travel north to Marksville on Louisiana Highway 1. The two towns are approximately five miles apart. Marksville is a pleasant small town with antebellum homes and hundreds of ancient live oak trees. At the center of Marksville at the Courthouse square, drive north a short distance on Louisiana Highway 107. Just north of town on the right side is Louisiana Highway 1192 and the Avoyelles Parish hospital. Turn right onto Louisiana Highway 1192. Travel approximately one-half mile until the road splits and take the right fork. Approximately 700 feet ahead on the left are the eroded ramparts of Fort DeRussy. This is the central portion of the small star fortress. The site is owned by the State of Louisiana, but it is undeveloped and has no amenities. You may walk up to the wall and take a short incline to see the interior of the bomb-proof or arsenal. Ahead and to the right are two obelisk markers. One is the grave of

Col. Lewis Gustave DeRussy, for whom the fort was named. The other obelisk is a memorial to slaves killed during the construction of the outer river works, which were part of the Ft. DeRussy complex.

If you drive a bit further over the plank bridge across Bayou Johnson, the road leads straight to the levee. If the gate is open, drive to the top of the levee. If not, it is easy to park your car and walk to it. If you turn and look back, the fort is still visible beyond the bayou. While still facing the fort look to the right. You will see a single line of trees that border two fields. These trees line the causeway (covered road) that led from the fort to a giant water battery. If you stand on the levee and face the fort, the water battery was located to your right and rear on a slight rise. If you face the water battery and look to the right and behind you, you will see the 1864 channel of the Red River. Water still fills a portion of it.

Retrace your route from DeRussy to Louisiana Highway 107. Turn right and follow 107 into Pineville, a distance of approximately 30 miles. In Pineville, take the Alexandria-Pineville Expressway and cross the Red River back into Alexandria. The expressway connects to I-49 in downtown Alexandria.

Grand Ecore: The next part of the tour will take you north into heart of the Red River Valley. Drive carefully; there are several twists and turns to get there! From Alexandria, drive on I-49 north 16 miles to the Boyce Exit (Exit 98). Cross

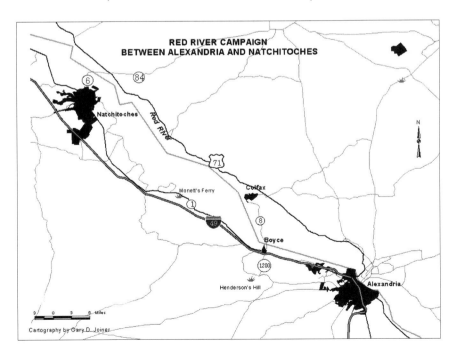

the Red River on Louisiana Highway 8 and travel north for approximately 11 more miles to the town of Colfax. There, take Louisiana Highway 490 (which skirts the town) and turn right onto the Louisiana Highway 490 Spur. Stay on this a short distance until you reach Louisiana Highway 158. Turn left on 158 and travel 2.5 miles to U.S. Highway 71. There, turn north onto U.S. Highway 71 for about 15 miles to the town of Clarence. At Clarence, turn left on Louisiana Highway 6 and travel about four miles to the Red River. When you cross the Louisiana Highway 6 bridge over the Red River, bluffs will be visible ahead on the opposite bank. On these bluffs was the village of Grand Ecore. On the left of the bridge a small rounded inlet marks the anchorage site of the Union fleet. On the right the cliff's highest points are more than 90 feet above the water.

These bluffs were fortified even before Louisiana entered the Union. Both Forts Seldon and Solubrity were located here. Ulysses S. Grant was stationed here for a short time during the Mexican War. The Confederates expanded the fortifications and General Banks's Union forces greatly increased their size immediately following his retreat from the battlefields of Mansfield and Pleasant

The bluffs at Grand Ecore.

Hill. The view from the bluffs is magnificent. *Carefully* park your car on the apron of the road and walk back to the top of the bluffs. Please note that there are no guardrails and the drop is sheer. *Be very careful and do not approach too closely to the edge.* Leave the apron (watch for traffic) and drive ahead to a sign that announces a shooting range. Take the road to the right and follow it along the bluff line. The irregular-looking ground formations you see are Union fortifications that protected and held 20,000 men until they could evacuate safely to Alexandria.

Retrace your path back to Louisiana Highway 6 and drive the short distance into Natchitoches. This city of colonial charm retains much of the French architecture from its earliest days. To return to I-49, proceed on the Louisiana Highway 6 By-Pass to Louisiana Highway 6 on the west side of the town, then turn right to connect with I-49 about four miles from the intersection.

Battle of Monett's Ferry (April 23, 1864): Turn left on I-49 and head south for about 18 miles to the Chopin Exit (Exit 119). You are now in the center of what was once the Battle of Monett's Ferry (or Cane River Crossing), fought on April 23, 1864. Drive left onto Louisiana Highway 490 a short distance to the Cane River. Cross it and continue on Louisiana Highway 490 to the intersection with Louisiana Highway 1 and turn right. This area is called Cane River Island, and is formed by the Cane and Red rivers.

The Union army was trapped here on its retreat from Natchitoches after its defeat at Mansfield and retreat from the battlefield at Pleasant Hill. There were only two ways to get off the island: march to the southern end and cross the Cane River at Monett's Ferry, or find a ford and cross the Cane River at a different spot. Confederate cavalry under Brig. Gen. Hamilton Bee tried to block the exit at the ferry, but his force was not of sufficient strength and Bee did not act as forcefully as the situation (and opportunity) demanded. Union troops found a ford and crossed troops to the west bank of the Cane, flanked Bee, and forced his retreat, thereby opening the ferry crossing to the rest of the Union army. Drive a short distance and cross the Cane River again. On the right side, just beside the bridge, was the ferry site. This battle (also called Cane River) was the last real opportunity the Confederates had to trap the Union forces during this important campaign.

Bailey's Dam: Turn around and retrace the path to I-49. Drive from the Chopin Exit to Alexandria ,a distance of 38 miles. There, near what is today the city's downtown river front park, Colonel Joseph Bailey constructed his amazing wing dam, which raised the level of the Red River enough to allow

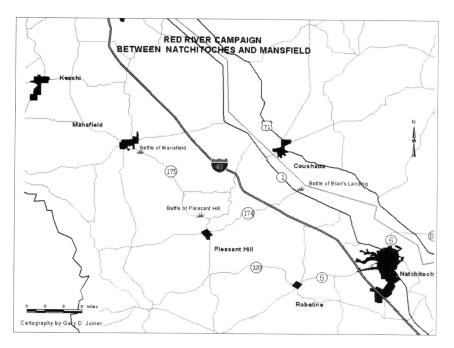

Porter's trapped fleet to pass over the rocky rapids to safety. Were it not for Bailey's ingenuity in early May 1864, it is virtually certain that Porter's entire flotilla would have been captured or destroyed. As one might imagine, little remains of Joe Bailey's remarkable dam.

The next part of the tour begins in Natchitoches. If you would like to follow the entire route of Banks's army, begin at Grand Ecore and retrace the route into Natchitoches. Follow Louisiana Highway 6 through town. Louisiana realigned 6 between Louisiana Highway 1 and I-49 several years ago, but the old road is still marked. Follow Highway 6 west to the town of Robeline, a distance of about 15 miles. Robeline was the site of White's store, located at the northeastern corner of the intersection of Louisiana Highway 6 and Louisiana Highway 120. Union soldiers dropped out of their column and bought everything in the small establishment on the trek north. During the retreat, they burned the store.

Follow the same route of the Union army by turning right onto Louisiana Highway 120 for approximately 15 miles to the junction of Louisiana Highway 175. This intersection is at the village of Bellmont, which in 1864 was called Crump's Corners. Turn right at the intersection of Louisiana Highway 175 and proceed another seven miles to Pleasant Hill. The present site of the town is in Sabine Parish. In 1864, the town was three miles farther north in DeSoto Parish.

The Battle of Mansfield (April 8, 1864): Mansfield was fought one day before the fighting at Pleasant Hill. It was the most important large-scale action of the campaign. It was also one of the last Confederate field victories of the war. The invading Union troops passed through Pleasant Hill toward Mansfield in their quest to reach Shreveport—and so shall we.

Union cavalry units encamped in the Pleasant Hill village on the night of April 6. The next morning Banks's column—stretching more than 20 miles—began moving north. The last marching units were just leaving Natchitoches and were strung out all along the road when disaster struck in the form of Richard Taylor's waiting Confederate army. Taylor's men first manifested themselves about three miles north of Pleasant Hill when Rebel horsemen checked advancing Union cavalry at Wilson's Farm. The skirmish bought time for Taylor's main body to prepare for battle just below Mansfield. A historic marker at Wilson's Farm on the left side of the road designates the center of that sharp but short engagement. Drive another seven miles. On the left is another historic marker identifying the location of Carroll's Mill, where Rebel cavalry once again slowed down the advancing Union column on the evening of April 7. Banks's army bivouacked along this road that night.

Continue another 10 miles on Louisiana Highway 175 to the Mansfield State Historic Site. Turn right at the gate and park at the visitor center to begin your tour. The small museum has a nice collection and the staff is knowledgeable and willing to help make your tour successful and enjoyable. The high ground upon which the visitor's center is located is called Honeycutt Hill, where the bloodiest fighting of the battle took place.

After you exit the Visitor's Center turn left and walk down the ridge line to the marker near the split rail fence by the highway. You are standing at the center of the Union line near the position of Nims's Federal Battery. Turn left and look down the road. On the morning of April 8, the Union army advanced from that direction toward where you are standing to take up its position on Honeycutt Hill. Taylor's Rebel army was in position behind you about one-half mile distant. If you face the road (with the visitor's center on your right), the Union line of battle ran straight through the museum to the bottom of the ridge. Behind you, the line ran across the road at sharp angle, through the brick house across the road and into the field behind it. Banks deployed his men in a tight L-shaped formation. Taylor's line was a wider crescent-shaped deployment. His Southerners assaulted the Union right flank first before hitting the left front and collapsing the entire position. Bank's troops lost all unit cohesion and bolted down the road to the south.

View of Honeycutt Hill (above) looking south toward the center of the Union line. (Below) Honeycutt Hill looking southeast along the road along which the Union army advanced to Mansfield. *Courtesy of the author*

When you are done visiting Mansfield, leave the visitor's center and turn left on to Louisiana Highway 175. Drive about one-third of a mile. On your right is a closed brick store at the intersection of Addison Road. Directly across from it is a driveway. This is the location of Sabine Crossroads, where the second phase of the fighting took place. Sabine Crossroads is another name for the Mansfield battle. The Union forces reformed and held this position for about twenty minutes before their line was again shattered and in retreat.

Drive ahead another two miles and on the left you will see the restored antebellum Allen House, which served as both General Banks's headquarters and as a field hospital. Another mile or so down the road on your left is a heavily mined area that designates the southernmost reaches of the Mansfield battlefield. Ahead of you looking south down the road is the sloping front of a large ridge, where the final fighting on the evening of April 8 took place. Chapman's Bayou, a stream that splits into two thin channels, cuts across the landscape. The Confederates pushed the Union forces across this creek and by doing so, denied them the only source of water available for several miles in every direction. After the sudden and stunning defeat at Mansfield, Banks decided to retreat to Pleasant Hill, where the second largest battle of the campaign was fought.

Pleasant Hill (April 9, 1864): It is now time to follow the route of Taylor's pursuit of Banks to Pleasant Hill. Retrace your route along Louisiana Highway 175 about seventeen miles to the original site of the village of Pleasant Hill. You will pass again the historical markers identifying the cavalry actions at Carroll's Mill and Wilson's Farm that preceded Mansfield. Drive another three miles to the intersection of Louisiana Highway 177. On your left once stood the Childers House, which served as General Banks's headquarters during the fighting on April 9. Turn around and drive north a short distance on Louisiana Highway 175. The battle of Pleasant Hill was fought along the straight stretch of road running ahead of you and around the far bend. Late on the afternoon Taylor launched a series of sharp assaults that battered Banks's army but did not drive him from the field as his attacks at Mansfield had done.

On the right side is an iron gateway. Drive through the gate and park. This land is owned by the Poimboeuf family, which has erected all of the historic granite interpretive markers. Put Louisiana Highway 175 behind you and you will see a large house in the distance. The original village of Pleasant Hill once stood in the open field between the house and where you are standing. Your position was the center of the Union line on April 9. Face to your left and look down the length of the field and you will see a small wooden house called a "dog-trot." This structure survived the battle and served as a hospital. The

This view at Pleasant Hill looks east from the center of the main Union line in the direction of the Confederate advance. *Courtesy of the author*

Confederates attacked across the field to your front left. Across the road and in front of you is the American Legion Hall. An old road can still be seen to the right of this building. Confederate Arkansas and Missouri troops under Brigadier General Thomas Churchill attempting to flank Banks's position reached the battlefield on this road. They mistakenly turned too soon and slammed into the Union left instead of behind it, as planned. Leave the parking area and turn right onto Louisiana Highway 175. On the left side where the road curves is a granite marker. Near this point Confederate Texas troops under Major General John G. Walker attacked and crushed that part of the Union line held by Colonel William T. Shaw. Ahead on your left is a large meadow that looks much as it did during the battle. Confederate artillery pounded Union positions from that point.

Blair's Landing (April 12, 1864): After Mansfield, Taylor ordered his cavalry to cut off the Union navy at Blair's Landing. Brig. Gen. Tom Green and 2,500 horsemen reached the landing on the afternoon of the 12th—before all of Porter's fleet had passed that point. What followed was a sharp and unique engagement between Rebel horsemen and Union tars.

To reach Blair's Landing, turn right or east onto Louisiana Highway 174 at Pleasant Hill, drive approximately 16 miles to its intersection with Louisiana

As far as we are aware, this is the first authentic published photograph of Blair's Landing, the site of Tom Green's cavalry battle with Porter's gunboats. The shifting river and other reasons made it difficult to confirm the exact location until recently. Green was killed in the foreground of this photo. *Courtesy Gary D. Joiner*

Highway 1, and turn left. Ahead a very short distance is another road that turns right and leads directly to the Red River Navigation System Lock and Dam 4. Follow this road to the lock and dam structure and park near the dam. The course of the river has changed since 1864. At the time of the battle the river here ran roughly perpendicular to its present course. The Texas cavalry was positioned on either side of the road you are now on. The Union navy vessels, including *U.S.S. Osage*, *U.S.S. Lexington*, and the transport *Black Hawk* passed directly in front from left to right. For about two hours Green's cavalry and four-gun artillery battery fired upon several warships and transports, without significant effect. Green was killed early in the action. Taylor reported only a handful of casualties, although a Federal report estimated Southern killed and wounded in the hundreds. Green's effort to capture, destroy, or prevent Porter's ships from retreating down river was unsuccessful.

Return to Louisiana Highway 1 and drive south into Natchitoches, a distance of 27 miles to conclude the tour of the most important sites in the Red River campaign.

Index